R. M. Collins

**Chapters from the Unwritten History of the War between the States**

The Incidents in the Life of a Confederate Soldier in Camp, on the March, in the Great Battles and in Prison

R. M. Collins

**Chapters from the Unwritten History of the War between the States**
*The Incidents in the Life of a Confederate Soldier in Camp, on the March, in the Great Battles and in Prison*

ISBN/EAN: 9783337307288

Printed in Europe, USA, Canada, Australia, Japan

Cover: Foto ©ninafisch / pixelio.de

More available books at **www.hansebooks.com**

# CHAPTERS

FROM THE

UNWRITTEN HISTORY

OF THE

# WAR BETWEEN THE STATES;

OR,

THE INCIDENTS IN THE LIFE OF A CONFEDERATE SOLDIER IN CAMP, ON THE MARCH, IN THE GREAT BATTLES, AND IN PRISON.

BY

LIEUT. R. M. COLLINS,

Co. B, 15TH TEXAS REGIMENT, GRANBURY'S BRIGADE, CLEBURNE'S DIVISION, ARMY OF TENNESSEE.

ST. LOUIS:
NIXON-JONES PRINTING CO.
1893.

TO THE MEMORY OF THE HEROES OF GRANBURY'S TEXAS BRIGADE, WHO WENT DOWN TO DEATH IN DEFENSE OF THEIR HOMES, AND TO THOSE WHO YET REMAIN ON THIS SIDE OF THE RIVER, THIS BOOK IS REVERENTLY AND AFFECTIONATELY INSCRIBED.

# CONTENTS.

| Chapter. | | Page. |
|---|---|---|
| I. | Getting ready to fight for our rights . . . | 9 |
| II. | From Clarksville, Texas, to Little Rock, Ark. . | 24 |
| III. | A Typical Mountaineer . . . . . . | 31 |
| IV. | A set-to with the 5th Kansas at Parikeet Bluff, Ark. . . . . . . . . . | 40 |
| V. | Ordered to Little Rock — Dismounted — Infantry drill — Camp Nelson — Ordered to Arkansas Post . . . . . . . . . | 60 |
| VI. | Battle of Arkansas Post . . . . . | 65 |
| VII. | After the surrender — A singing match — On board boats . . . . . . . . | 71 |
| VIII. | Trip up the great river — One of our men shot by the guard at Belmont, Mo. . . . . | 78 |
| IX. | At Columbus, Ohio — Lunched by Mrs. A. G. Thurman — In prison . . . . . | 85 |
| X. | Governors Todd, Bright and Andy Johnson visit our prison — Removed from Camp Chase to Ft. Delaware . . . . . . . . | 93 |
| XI. | From Pittsburg to Ft. Delaware — At Philadelphia on Sunday — Mad and mobbishly disposed Quakers . . . . . . . . | 102 |
| XII. | On our way to Dixie — Sea-sickness — Exchanged at City Point . . . . . . . | 112 |
| XIII. | At Richmond, Va. — Our new suit . . . | 120 |
| XIV. | At the home of our boyhood — Some Tennessee girls knock a ton of conceit out of us with a bouquet . . . . . . . . | 126 |
| XV. | At Tulahoma and Wartrace, Tenn. — Bragg's retreat . . . . . . . . | 133 |

## CONTENTS.

| Chapter. | | Page. |
|---|---|---|
| XVI. | Tennessee moonshiner — Chickamauga campaign opens | 139 |
| XVII. | Bragg abandons Chattanooga — McLemore's Cove failure | 147 |
| XVIII. | The battle of Chickamauga | 154 |
| XIX. | A day on the field of Chickamauga after the battle | 160 |
| XX. | Six weeks in front of Chattanooga — Hell's Half Acre | 167 |
| XXI. | Battle of Missionary Ridge | 174 |
| XXII. | Retreat — Battle of Ringgold Gap | 184 |
| XXIII. | Winter of '63 at Tunnel Hill — Miss Mary A. H. Gay | 192 |
| XXIV. | Battle with snow-balls — Another furlough — The Georgia campaign | 200 |
| XXV. | The terrific battle of New Hope Church | 209 |
| XXVI. | Pine and Kenesaw Mountains — Gen. Johnston removed — Gen. Hood succeeds him. | 217 |
| XXVII. | Hood goes on the war-path — Battle of Peach Tree Creek | 227 |
| XXVIII. | Hood's Tennessee campaign — Spring Hill failure — The battle of Franklin | 239 |
| XXIX. | Battle of Nashville, Tenn.— Disastrous results — The retreat — Kicking Jim and us | 250 |
| XXX. | Gen. Cheatham — Crossed the Tennessee — Our boats — Ordered to North Carolina — The boys do up Montgomery on the way | 264 |
| XXXI. | From Montgomery, Ala., to Bentonville, N. C. | 277 |
| XXXII. | In the swamps about Bentonville — Find a barrel of brandy | 289 |
| XXXIII. | The last days of the Confederacy — On our way home — Wreck, narrow escape | 300 |
| XXXIV. | Another wreck — From Nashville to New Orleans — Have a royal time in the grand old city | 311 |
| XXXV. | Broke bread and eat salt with Doctor Hamilton and Miss Sallie — Home | 322 |

# PREFACE.

To send forth this book to the reading public without some sort of preface would be doing violence to a very ancient custom, "a custom more honored in the observance than in the breach." We did not write this book for pleasure nor pastime, but to contribute our mite in the direction of getting into cold type that part of the history of the great war between the States, from 1861 to 1865, that is recorded only in the memories of the men and officers of the line, and if we succeed in entertaining the reader for an hour or two in our descriptions of great battles or pathetic scenes incident to the life of a soldier, or cause a smile to dance on the face of the old or young, like sunlit shadows chasing each other on the wavelets of a mountain lake, we will have done well.

THE AUTHOR.

# CHAPTER I.

## MAKING UP A COMPANY AND GETTING READY TO "FIGHT FOR OUR RIGHTS."

In the month of February, 1862, the clash of arms and the tramp of mailed warriors came ringing down through the valleys of the Indian Territory, and struck the young American of North Texas full in the face. The Confederates under Gen. Ben McCulloch, and the Federals under Gen. S. R. Curtis, were having a regular set-to, and the idea of the Yankees heading for Texas soil to despoil our fair homes, insult our women and eat up the substance of the people was just a little more than we proposed to submit to.

Decatur, our home, was quite a small town then, and Wise County had only about 200 voters, and all those who were not school teachers or clerks in stores were cowboys. G. B. Pickett was commissioned to raise a company, and then commenced the rushing to and fro getting things in shape to enlist, go to the wars and get honor, glory and some immortality. The day was set Saturday for the enrolling of names and organization of the company, and in they came on their little fingertail, frosty-necked, calico Spanish ponies, all clamorous to get into the cavalry service. A company of a hundred men was made up. G. B. Pickett was elected Captain, Tom Roberson 1st, W. A. King 2nd and F. J. Barrett 3rd Lieutenants. Of the non-commissioned officers we only remember a big red-headed fellow by the name of G. W. Rodgers, a school teacher, who was made Orderly Sergeant. After the organization, and lots of Dexter's best had been put under their jackets, the remainder of the day was put in in cavalry movements round and round the Public Square.

While the company was made up of a very nice lot of young men, boys and middle-aged men, it did not strike us as having very much the appearance of N. Bonaparte's Old Guard. The writer was a clerk in the dry goods store of Howell & Allen, and had not put his name down yet. In fact, he felt much disposed to await developments before putting himself in a position to be offered up on the altar of our young Confederacy. Fact is, we had the post-office in our house, and had free access to such papers as the New York Tribune, New York Herald, Missouri Republican, Brownlow's Knoxville Whig, Louisville Journal, Cincinnati Times, etc., and we read them all. We also read the speeches of the Southern members in Congress and Ben Wade's great speech, and we felt it in our very bones that there was going to be a big fight and lots of people hurt and hurt badly; and besides all this, the Southern States only had about eight million people, and four million of these were negroes, while the Northern States had about eight million white folks, and in figuring on it we could not figure out how we were going to whip two to one; and in addition to all this, we did not then and do not to this good day, believe in the doctrine of peaceable secession of any of the States, but we believed in the right to rebel, and this explains why we will in so many places in these reminiscences refer to the Confederates as rebels. We were a rebel simple and pure, and expected when the war ended to be treated as such by the United States government.

But we must quit this line and get back into the unwritten history. It is that field we propose to cultivate for our own amusement as well as that of our friends.

After the organization of our company until the order to march was received all hands were busy getting things in shape to take the field, and the people either from pure patriotism, or fear of the consequences of resistance, opened their doors to the boys. Merchants piled out their clothing, hats, boots and shoes, and men owning herds of horses were willing to give them up, so that it was only a few days until all the boys were mounted. The martial spirit seemed to have drowned out all other spirits except Dexter's best. Music was in the air. Every young lady in town and country was warbling the "Bonnie Blue Flag," "Dixie" and the "Secession Wagon" as sweetly as mocking birds.

As to arms to fight with, the variety in kind, caliber and quality, is beyond our powers of description. Some had double-barrelled and some had single barrelled shot-guns; some had squirrel rifles and some had the old buck and ball muskets. In one thing only were all armed alike, and that was with big knives. These were made for us by the blacksmiths, out of old scythe blades, plowshares, cross cut saws, or anything else that could be had. The blade was from two to three feet in length, and ground as sharp as could be. The scabbards for these great knives were, as a rule, made of raw hide, with the hairy side out, and they were worn on the belt like a sword, and doubtless many trees in the pine forests over in Arkansas show to this day the marks of these knives, for we used to mount our ponies and gallop through pine thickets, cutting the tops from young pine trees, practicing so that we could lift the heads of the Yankees artistically as soon as we could catch up with them.

About the first of March, 1862, orders were received for the company to report at once at Dallas. After remaining there some weeks it moved up to McKinney. Here the 15th Texas Cavalry was organized by electing Geo. H. Sweet, of San Antonio, Colonel; W. K. Mastin, of Dallas, Lieutenant-Colonel, and W. H. Cathey, of Denton, Major. About the 10th of March the regiment was ordered to report at Camp McKnight, near Clarksville, Texas.

On the 15th of March the war fever as well as the fear that the ladies would present us with a hoop skirt struck the writer and ran his pulse up to 185 to the minute in the shade, and Capt. G. B. Pickett swore us into the Confederate service for one year. We put in about ten days getting in fighting trim. We were confronted first by the difficulty of procuring arms. We rustled up an old gun barrel that had doubtless served its time as a squirrel rifle, as it ran about 120 bullets to the pound. Amos Grider stocked it for us, and we had him train it all distances as far as it would reach, with the wind, against the wind and at right angles to the wind. The barrel was about four and a half feet long, and the pecan ramrod was about fifteen inches longer than the barrel, and kinked downward at the end like we have seen a dog do his tail when suffering from the effects peculiar to and bordering on the ragged edge between a shy and a wild. Uncle Amos, as he was called, was not only a cunning worker in wood but was nearly related to old Vulcan and therefore, we had him make our big knife. On the morning of March 25th, W. C. Burris, H. H. Gaines, Dude George and the writer left Decatur bound for our command at Clarksville. Pretty soon after we arrived at Camp McKnight the regiment was moved to a camp some three miles east of Clarksville. Miss Belle Gordon, a pretty young lady, lived immediately on the road from our camp to the city. She was a fine performer on the piano, and as hers was the first instrument of the kind the boys had ever seen they kept her playing night and day. In our mind's eye we can see her yet as she paws the ivory and sings the "Bonnie Blue Flag," with her great brown eyes turned towards that country where good soldiers all go.

Our days at Clarksville, when it was not raining, were spent very pleasantly. The variety was fairly good — some company drill, some regimental drill, and some guard duty. Rev. J. W. P. McKinzie preached to us several times. He was a grand man, but like a majority of the preachers of that day, he was on the fight. While here, from some cause, our regiment was reorganized. Our Captain, G. B. Pickett, was made Major, Lieut. Flavius J. Barrett was promoted to the Captaincy of our company. A. Faulkner, now Gen. Passenger and Ticket Agent for M. K. and T. Railway, was elected Captain of Company "G," beating Dr. Harper, of Denton County. Capt. Faulkner had been in the State only about one year prior to the war, hailing from the State of New York, but he was a sound Democrat, a rebel through and through, a fine specimen of young American manhood, and as brave as Julius Cæsar or any other of the Cæsar boys — a perfect specimen of an American volunteer soldier.

The following account of the presentation of an elegant silk banner to his company, by the beautiful and accomplished Miss Ida De Morse, is quoted from the Clarksville (Texas) Standard of April 18, 1862 :—

CAMP PICKETT, April 17, 1862.

*Editor Clarksville Standard:*

The company commanded by Capt. Faulkner, Col. Sweet's regiment, was on Saturday last at their battalion ground, and in the presence of some eight or ten hundred spectators, complimented by the young ladies of Clarksville with a handsome company flag. A circumstance of which we all feel not a little proud, and of which we desire the world in general, and our friends at home in particular, to be apprised. At the special request of the subscriber, Miss Ida De Morse and Captain Faulkner have furnished us with the addresses delivered upon the occasion, and if you will give them place in the columns of your valuable paper you will confer upon our company a very appreciable favor.

Respectfully,

D. L. McGARY,
*Orderly Sgt. Faulkner's Co.*

### MISS IDA DE MORSE'S ADDRESS.

*Gentlemen and Soldiers:*

This is no ordinary occasion, and it is with no common feelings that I appear before you, a band of brave and gallant men, to present to you the emblem of our country's nationality and independence, beneath whose folds you are to conquer peace or fill a warrior's grave. The records of the past justly boast that "Thermopylæ had her messenger of death; the Alamo had none." You have a character to sustain, and a reputation to support — a Mc-

Culloch, a Travis, a Terry, and a host of God-like dead, whose actions we expect you to imitate, whose names you must never sully.

The banner I present to you to-day is the banner of a people struggling to be free from the most loathsome despotism that ever was sought to be imposed upon a people who know their rights and knowing, dare maintain them.

For the achievement of our independence you have torn yourself from those ties intimately connected and interwoven with the affections of the heart, perhaps imprinted the last kiss upon the lips of your cherished child — clasped to a crushed heart the form of a devoted wife, and cast one longing, lingering glance to a home that is your pride, and laid yourselves upon your country's altar, peradventure a voluntary sacrifice in the cause of freedom. If the prayers of woman, will avail with the God of battle, to guard and protect in the hour of danger, and restore you to the embraces of those your heart holds dear, if our sympathies and tears, can cheer and nerve a soldier's heart, ours shall be thine. We are a people that can never be conquered when such sacrifices are made for the maintenance of our infant republic — future generations will deify you, and your names will be a glorious legacy to those that follow you.

Take then this banner, make it virtually the banner of the free, follow it into the very jaws of destruction; either to a glorious death or a glorious victory, and if counted amid the unreturning braves, make it your martial cloak without regret, and proudly fill a warrior's grave, die with your face to the foe and with the exclamation that —

> If there be on this earthly sphere
> A boon or gift that heaven holds dear,
> 'Tis the last libation that liberty draws
> From the heart that bleeds and breaks in her cause.

While it breaks our hearts to see you leave we bid you Godspeed on this glorious errand. Our prayers will follow you and our tears will encircle your pathway wherever you go. All that we demand in return is that you —

> Strike till the last armed foe expires,
> Strike for our altars and our fires,
> Strike for the green graves of our sires,
> God and our native land.

## CAPTAIN FAULKNER'S RESPONSE.

*Miss Ida De Morse:*

I am not much accustomed to public speaking, nor can I express my feelings on this occasion. But for myself and my company, from the depths of my heart, I thank you for this beautiful flag. We are, as you have truly said, a band of brethren, just entering upon a perilous campaign, but in defense of as sacred a cause as ever engaged the energies of a nation, and the knowledge that we bear with us the sympathies of the kind and beautiful of our land, will but nerve our arms for harder blows so long as we remain upon the field of action. But in the fullness of sincerity, I pledge you that just so long as the minions of that northern government, which has threatened our people with the chains of bondage, shall continue to desecrate our soil with their footprints, just so long shall this Bonnie Blue Flag continue to wave over the heads of our brave men. And rather than permit it, for a moment, to hang trailing in the dust, or see its beautiful folds stained with dishonor, it shall be dyed with the best blood that "chambers in our hearts."

If recent advices from the seat of war be reliable, already has the clash of arms been heard ringing through the great valley of the Father of Waters. Thousands of the northern foe now lie clasped in the cold embrace of death, other thousands have surrendered their arms and as prisoners in the hands of our brave brethren, are now begging for that mercy which they in the hour of their temporary success seem never to have remembered. The Genius of Victory is once more with the banner of the South.

So may it ever be. Other engagements must soon follow, and it is devoutly wished that our regiment may be allowed to participate. For—

> Never lovelorn youth in lady's bower,
> Did pant for the appointed hour
> As we, until before us stand
> The Lincoln leaders and their band.

And now, Miss Ida, hoping that when this grim-visaged war shall have smoothed its "wrinkled front," when the war hounds of Lincoln shall have been driven back to their northern kennels, and when our country rearing her proud crest amongst the greatest of earth's powers, shall be recognized and acknowledged as the chosen guardian of the ark of human liberty, that to us may be permitted a return to our homes, and a re-union in peace with the loved ones we leave behind. For myself and for the troop I have the honor to command, I again tender to you our sincere thanks for this Bonnie Blue Flag.

While at Clarksville the 12th, 14th, 16th, 17th and 18th Texas regiments of cavalry arrived. And when these six regiments, six thousand in all, were strung out in line of battle on the prairie, it just appeared to our boy eyes that we had men enough to whip the United States, with Canada and Mexico thrown in for good count, and we were really uneasy for fear the rebels would clean up the Yankees before we got a taste of the war. Us boys were all puffed up as to our numbers, and it was no uncommon thing to hear some of them in camps giving such commands as "Attention, World! By nations right wheel into line, m-a-r-c-h!" At the beginning of the war young Texas in the saddle was regarded as a whole set put together in thirds, one-third man and bell spurs, one-third gun, pistol and knife, and one-third pony.

## CHAPTER II.

MARCH FROM CLARKSVILLE, TEXAS, TO LITTLE ROCK, ARKANSAS — REORGANIZATION AND RAID INTO IZZARD COUNTY.

About the 10th of April orders were received for our command to move at once to Corinth, Miss. The great battle of Shiloh, as called by the Confederates, and by the Federals the battle of Pittsburg Landing, having been fought, resulting disastrously to the Confederates. We moved at once, and the march from Clarksville, Texas, to Pine Bluff, Ark., with such a large body of raw cavalry, was a pretty rough introduction into the pomp and circumstance of so called glorious war. It rained on us quite every day during the march, and as each company had from two to four wagons, in which the extra trumpery of the soldiers was transported, our train was a big thing to move, to say nothing of six thousand raw, green and exacting Texans, mounted on horses that knew about as much about how to shift and make the best of a soldier's life as they did. The rivers were all up booming, and the roads were simply bottomless. We remained some days at Pine Bluff. The clouds rolled away, and an Arkansas April sun came out, and besides affording us an opportunity to dry our clothing and bedding, it dried the rawhide scabbards of our big knives, rendering them worthless, because they fit as tight as the bark on a black jack, and were as hard to draw as a nigger's eye teeth. We threw them in the Arkansas River. After a few days we were moved up to Little Rock, and went into camp out near St. John's College. By this time the measles had broken out in camps, and the supply seemed to be sufficient to go round. While here another reorganization of our command became necessary, because of the Confederate conscript law, which let out all over thirty-five and under eighteen years of age. In this election Maj. G. B. Pickett was made Lieutenant-Colonel, Geo. H. Sweet was re-elected Colonel, and W. H. Cathay was made Major of the 15th Texas Cavalry, and W. C. Burris and the writer were elected lieutenants of Company "B," vice W. A. King and

Tom Robertson, who were let out and went home to Texas, by reason of being over thirty-five years of age.

About May the 15th, Gen. T. C. Hindman, an ex-member of Congress from the State of Arkansas, was made a Major-General and put in command of all the troops west of the Mississippi. His first order on taking command was to burn all the cotton on the Arkansas River; and for days the black smoke from the burning cotton bales all up and down the river ascended towards heaven as a burnt offering to the gods of war, and the folly of a foolish people, who thought that cotton was king, and that by burning it and keeping it as much as possible out of the hands of the Yankees, they would be forced to acknowledge the independence of the Southern Confederacy, just as if the world was dependent on the Southern States for material out of which to make clothing. This was about as foolish as passing a law exempting from service in the army all those who were owners of so many negro slaves. While at Little Rock the service was light, as we were not required to drill nor do much guard duty. About the middle of June a big St. Peter burley-looking

Arkansas Brigadier-General by the name of Rust, was put in command of our six regiments of Texas cavalry and ordered on a raid up towards Batesville, where the Yankee army was, under command of General Curtis. Our command consisted of the 12th Texas Cavalry, commanded by Col. W. H. Parsons; 14th, commanded by Col. M. T. Johnson; 15th, by Col. Geo. H. Sweet; 16th, by Col. Bill Fitzhugh; 17th, by Col. Taylor, and 18th by Col. Darnell. At Searcy was the first sign we struck of the ravages of war. A small command of Yankee cavalry had been on a raid that far down and had been sailed into by some Texas cavalry. They had torn down some fencing and burned a few dwellings. It seemed strange to us that a civilized people would have so little respect for other people's property as to destroy it in that way, but we learned later on that war meant not only to kill, but to destroy property. On we go as jolly as larks, confident that we had the biggest army in the world. Fact is, five thousand Texas cavalry strung out did make a long line, when the fact is considered that each pony had not only to have walking room in the road, but had to have plenty of kicking room, to say nothing of the room required for our long squirrel rifles and ramrods. At Col. Kemper's on Flat Woods, in Izzard County, we struck a country where the Federals had been foraging around and the citizens commenced gathering in and telling us what they had done in the way of taking their corn, wheat, horses and so on, and the bristles commenced to raise on our backs and we were all hot under our collars and just spoiling for a fight. Some local scouts came in and reported a party of Federals some twenty miles away, across White River, threshing wheat. General Rust took five regiments and went down toward Batesville and crossed the river with a view of cutting them off, while Col. Sweet, with the 15th Regiment, marched down Rocky Comfort with orders to remain on the river at the mouth of this creek until further orders were received. We arrived at this point about sundown. The citizens reported the Federals just across the river. Col. Sweet called a council of all his captains and lieutenants to take a vote on disobeying orders and crossing the river and taking in this outfit of Federals. We all voted to disobey orders, cross over the river and sail into them. It was very dark. Our guide piloted the head of our column down to the river and then up the road quite a half mile to a shoal where we could ford it, and then down the other side to a point opposite where we had gone in. The water between the going in and going out places was deep enough to float a steamboat. On we go quietly expecting every minute to find them. All at once the head of our column met an obstruction and the word was whispered down the line: "Here they are," but it turned out to be our own men, General Rust having crossed the river and was coming up on the other side. As soon as we found out the situation the head of our column was turned and recrossed the river, but quite a number of our out-fit thought Rust's command were Yankees and that we were retreating and were too much scared to make the circuit around the deep water and went straight across. It was a miracle how they all got out, but their ponies seemed to swim like fish. We camped there all night and returned to Flat Woods next day, crossing the limpid waters of Rocky Comfort one hundred and thirty-three times in going twenty miles, and nine out of every ten of our horses were barefooted. The outfit of Federals doubtless heard of our coming and made good their escape to Batesville. Gen. Rust with all the command except about one hundred and fifty of our regiment returned to the neighborhood of Little Rock. We were left for the purpose of keeping our eyes on Gen. Curtis' command and preventing it from foraging over the country. Now Izzard county is a broken mountainous country and the people were as ancient, simple and honest as were the citizens of East Tennessee a half century ago. Men, boys, old women and pretty rosy-cheeked girls all went barefooted alike. The exception to the rule was to find a family that put on anything like style. They were all agreed that a Texas cavalryman was a hero. Irish potatoes, and chickens, were ripe and for good milk and butter it was many furlongs in the lead of any country we struck during the war. We had a royal time while it lasted. We were cut off from the world and had no conception of what was in store for us in the next two years, but we put in all the bird-singing month of June in rollicking around over them high mountains, living high and making love to them pretty, honest Arkansaw girls.

## CHAPTER III.

A TYPICAL MOUNTAINEER OF THOSE DAYS — A DASH INTO KNIGHT'S COVE — ATTACK ON GEN. CURTIS' OUTPOST AT BATESVILLE.

One bright Sunday afternoon our scouts came in and reported a party of Federals cutting and stacking wheat in Knight's Cove, some twelve or fifteen miles away, down on the river in the direction of Batesville.

Now Knight's Cove is one of those picturesque little valleys nestling among the hills of Arkansas, which the people of those delightfully rural retreats called "coves." It belonged to a man named Knight, and he was supposed to be a Union man. The cove or valley occupied about 500 acres, had all been planted in wheat, and the Yankees had gone in there and cut and stacked it and were getting ready to begin threshing. We dashed into the cove by fours, or like a goat goes to war, but we were again doomed to disappointment.

The Federals had gone, and we were just about ready to conclude that the war would come to an end before we got a taste of the fight, and that we would have to return home without any honorable scars, laurels, bruised arms, or anything to tell as to how we had cleaned up the Yankees, horse, foot and dragoon.

About this time Capt. A. Faulkner, commanding Company G, found himself afoot, but being a young man of infinite resources, he did not remain in that fix many days. He secured leave of absence, borrowed one of the boy's horses, and lit out hunting for somebody who had one to sell. Away over across the river a very enthusiastic, well-to-do Union man lived, and while he lived very near the Federal lines, yet the Captain went to see him and made himself very agreeable, faring on the best grub and drink the old fellow could put up, all the while playing that he was a Federal captain and belonged to the Union army at Batesville. This was honor enough for the old Union fellow. His cup of joy was full, and he was prolific in all sorts of hard stories about the meanness of the rebels in his section. The Captain played him up to the right point, and before any of his strings played him false he suggested to the old fellow that he was quite afoot, and that the happy thing would be for him to sell him a good horse. The old gentleman jumped at the opportunity to do a patriotic deed, and ordered his fine black stallion brought out — a really magnificent animal. Faulkner agreed at once to the price asked, gave him a voucher on the Federal Quartermaster at Batesville, threw himself into the saddle, and did not stand on the order of his going, but went at once. The deception was a success, and was right, because in war, and for the good of the State.

Captain Faulkner being mounted now, to a queen's taste, and being a restless, industrious soldier, suggested to Col. Sweet that he be permitted to select fifty choice men from the command, and those best mounted, and organize a rifle company. To this the Colonel readily agreed, for notwithstanding Col. Sweet had all along in every way possible done all in his power to retard Faulkner's advancement, he was being forced to recognize in him the elements of a successful soldier. He had the dash of a Francis Marion, the courage of a mad Anthony Wayne, and the power to impart it to men under his command, and had his lot been cast in the army of Tennessee or Virginia, he would have come out of the army a Major-General. Like all soldiers, he held that a man would not die nor be killed in the army until his time came.

The service we were doing for the Confederacy was too tame for our hot Texas blood, and the boys were clamorous for a set-to and a closer acquaintance with the Yankees and their prowess in battle. Something had to be done. We were fat, sleek, and full to running over with fight. So one bright Sunday morning about the 20th of June, Col. Sweet called us into line and made us a speech. He said: "We have been waltzing up and down these mountains, across these valleys, eating new Irish potatoes and spring chickens just long enough, and we are going to punish the enemy this very day, even if we have to go right into Batesville and pull old Gen. Curtis' beard till he gets mad enough to entertain us in a war-like manner." At this the boys all yelled. The writer was detailed and put in command of fifteen men as an advance guard, with orders to keep from a half to three-quarters of a mile in advance, and off we moved on a kind of country road right down the backbone of a rocky, huckleberry, chestnut mountain, towards the enemy. Our advance guard out-traveled the command, we halted under the shade of a grand old chestnut tree and threw our leg over our pony's neck to rest. In our front was a log cabin, with only two holes in it, the "front" door and chimney. It was surrounded by a four-rail fence. Down across the road, on the mountain side, was the calf pen. The old man came out, and he was a full-grown specimen of a mountain boomer. We at once recognized him as the prototype of the kind we had seen browsing around loose on the spurs of the Blue Ridge, in one of the upper counties of East Tennessee. He was of the regulation build, red-headed, freckled faced and "heavy sot." His shirt and pants were the fruit of the home loom; his suspenders were knit of yarn; bare-headed and bare-footed, with his shirt bosom spread wide open, he was a breathing, moving personification of don't-care frankness and honesty. After the greetings of the day, says he: "Whose 'critter' company is this, and who commands it?" We told him that we were Texas cavalry, that we were in command and enjoyed the honor of being a

Lieutenant in the army. "Well," says he, "Leftenant, I am glad to see you. Say, old woman, and you gals, all of you come out here, these are Texicans." They all came, the old lady and five red-headed girls. "Well, Leftenant, is thar anything on this hill you want? If thar is name it," remarked the old man. We told him that we would like some good, cold buttermilk and cornbread. He turned to one of the girls and said, "Bring the Leftenant what he wants, and do it quick." The girl cleared the fence at one bound, and came back with a cedar "piggin" full of buttermilk and her apron full of corn dodgers. The white staves and red staves and long handle of the piggin looked nice and clean, but the half melted butter floating around on top of the milk, and the long-handled gourd we had to drink it out of made it pretty hard to eat so early in the war. We noticed a smile come over the face of our boys when we invited them to help themselves, and they refused, leaving the writer to get out of it the best way he could. We sailed into it, and did our level best to show the good people that we appreciated their hospitality. We soon got enough, and with the excuse that our command was approaching, we took our leave.

About twelve o'clock we arrived at a mill, on a bright, clear running creek near Batesville. Col. Sweet formed a part of his little command into a half-moon shape about the mill, placed the balance in ambush along the side of the road, and dispatched Capt. Tom Johnson with a squad of men to take in the Federal outpost, which was stationed about a quarter of a mile further on the road towards Batesville. This they were only partially successful in, killing two, the others making their escape into the city. The firing of the guns or the report made by those Federals who escaped, created no little stir in the great Federal army. The blast of trumpets and the long roll of drums was simply terrific. This was the first demonstration we had struck that there were lots of people on the other side ready for fight, and we felt relieved when our Colonel gave the command to mount and vacate that region at once, and we lit out on what is called in military parlance double quick time, right up the road over which we had come in hot haste seeking whom we might devour. It was some time next day when some of us landed back at Knight's Cove.

About the first of July Gen. Curtis moved his army down White River to Jacksonport. As soon as he was safely out of the way our command moved down and dashed into the city, with heads up and tails over the dash board, Col. Sweet at the head of our column, dressed in full uniform, with nice silk sash, and mounted on a fine charger. The citizens, as a rule, seemed glad to see us.

We went into camp over south of the river, in a grand beach and maple grove near a big blue spring. After a few days our scouts came in and reported a train of eight suttler wagons, unguarded, traveling on the road to Curtis' army, at Jacksonport. A detachment was sent out and brought them in. It proved to be a rich capture, as they were all loaded to the guards with fancy bottled wet groceries, ginger cakes, sardines, oysters, calico, ladies' hoop skirts, spool thread, boots, shoes, tobacco, etc. We opened up the outfit at camp, each fellow appropriating what he wanted, and a great many things we did not need, for the writer owns up to drinking so many sardines and eating so much Martel brandy, that we have had an abiding prejudice against both ever since. The overplus of dry goods, boots, shoes, hats, thread, etc., Col. Sweet ordered distributed among the citizens, and you can bet we boys were the pie crust with those Arkansas girls as long as the hoop skirts, spool cotton and calico lasted. Pretty women just swarmed to our camp, nice balls and parties over in the city were all the go, and we just thought if this was all that war meant, by being a Confederate soldier we had struck rich paying dirt, and we didn't care if it lasted a couple of score of years; but a few days after this quite a different taste was put in our mouths.

## CHAPTER IV.

COL. CLAYTON'S 5TH KANSAS GIVE US OUR FIRST WHIFF OF GUNPOWDER — WE RUN 18 MILES TO CATCH THEM, AND THEN RUN 18 MILES TO LET THEM LOOSE.

While here five printers belonging to Company "A," from San Antonio, Taylor Thompson, his brother Henry C. Thompson, H. C. Logan, Billy Schott and Lieut. G. B. Hathaway, took charge of the Batesville Eagle office, a Union newspaper that had been abandoned by the proprietor when Curtis' army left, and got out a scorching, red-hot secession paper and mailed it to the subscribers as their names appeared on the books. Those old Union fellows came biling in, paid off their subscriptions and ordered their paper stopped. The boys replenished their exchequer to the tune of about eighty dollars, pied the office, and left it alone in its glory.

On Sunday morning, July 8th, while most our

A. Faulkner
Capt Comdg Co G
15th Texas Cavalry
C S A

command was performing the sad duty of putting Jack Spraddling in his grave, who had been accidentally shot the day before, our scouts came dashing into camp, covered with dust and their horses foaming with perspiration. We knew they had heard or seen something that they were just dying to tell, and sure enough they reported having discovered a big wagon train of supplies a few miles away, on the road to Curtis' army, and guarded by only 200 of Col. Clayton's 5th Kansas cavalry. Col. Sweet decided at once that this was a spread just our size, and the capture of 200 Yankees and a big train of wagons filled with good supplies, caused visions of glory, honor and a Brigadier-General's commission all to pass in rapid succession before his eyes, and before the sound of his voice in giving the command, "Attention, Battalion!" had been wafted away on the wind and whispered through the sugar tree and beach leaves on the great trees in the river bottom, the boys were getting into line. The writer was afoot, our horse having the foot evil, but we soon struck a dicker with James L. Harding, of the Wise County Company, and secured his horse. By one o'clock we were off with the rifle company commanded by Capt. Faulkner, in the advance. As we passed up through the main street of the city, the ladies were all out in their Sunday-go-to-meeting goods, and were waving their handkerchiefs at us, and the way we did yell! We were halted in front of a fine brick hotel where there was quite a crowd of citizens. Col. Sweet made one of his spread-eagle speeches, winding up with his favorite expression, "We are going to punish the enemy." On we go, up hill, down dale, through valleys, lanes, woodland, and by fine old farms. When not in a lope our horses were on a dead run. The day was hot, the weather dry and the roads dusty, and while there were only about 100 in our command, we raised a terrible dust, which settled on our sweaty selves and horses, giving us the appearance of a hard, dirty set.

About half a mile from Parikeet Bluff, on the classic banks of Black river, we struck the enemy's pickets and captured them, and while detailing a guard to hold them Captain Faulkner commanding the advance guard, took in the lay of the country and position of the enemy, and suggested to Col. Sweet, that the command be dismounted and go into the fight as infantry, that the idea of men armed with squirrel rifles, shot-guns and muzzle-loading pistols, going into battle on horseback was preposterous in the extreme, but the Colonel refused to take the advice, and ordered the advance guard to charge, and at them we went in columns of four, or like a gentleman sheep goes to war — red hot from the heat on the outside, and red hot inside for a fight. At least two-thirds of the Federals had crossed the river. To the left of the road on which we went at them was a deep ravine, on the right a high fence; just to the right of the road and near the river bank, was a blacksmith shop, and some seventy yards yet to our right stood an old-fashioned two-story frame dwelling, and in the rear of our right were some out-houses, stables, barns, etc. Captain Tom Johnson was killed at the first fire by a big, fat Dutchman. Tom Teague, a very close friend of Captain Johnson, shot the Dutchman dead, putting the muzzle of his gun so close to him that it set his clothing on fire. Captain Faulkner's fine horse was killed under him, but he supplied himself at once from Federal horses hitched about the blacksmith shop.

We went at them with such a whirlygust and yell, that the Kansas fellows seemed kind o' appalled and hid out, and we had things our own way for a few minutes. But those fellows across the river were the first to recover and commenced pouring a deadly fire into us from their carbines and six-shooters. By this time the Federals in the houses, barns and stables, and about the blacksmith shop and in the ravine to our left, spit on their hands and came at us. Fact is, our outfit had less than a quarter of an acre of room to fight on, while the Federals were comfortably fixed as to room, protection and numbers, and they poured it into us from front, rear and both flanks. It was an exceedingly hot place for about ten minutes. Col. Sweet's horse was killed under him.

The writer was on the extreme right of our line, about the blacksmith shop. Just east of the shop there stood a new striped Kansas wagon, with sheet on, and on the seat sat a very pretty young woman. She seemed to be spellbound at what was going on about her. We discovered a man on the other side of the wagon, and about the same time he discovered us. He stepped out and we took a fair pop at each other and both missed. He stepped so as to put the wagon between us, and as the sheet lacked some inches of reaching the wagon bed, we saw him loading his carbine. We knew that the chances were at the next pop he would get us. We called to George W. Ross, of Faulkner's company, who was getting in his work on some Federals down near the ferry, to help catch that fellow. George swung his long double-barreled shot-gun around to get it in range with the fellow, and as he did so the gun went off. This seemed to alarm him and he ran for a thicket of brush just to the right. We shot at him as he ran, but have no idea we hit him. He was a tall, handsome, dark-skinned young man, and the woman in the wagon may have been his wife; anyway he made a brave fight for her.

This was the last load we had in our pistol; our caps, powder and balls were loose in our saddlebags, along with a deck of cards, hence we had nothing to do but to sit on our horse, look on and wait to be killed, or for the command to run to be given. We rode up to where Lieut. W. O. Yantis, of Tarrant county, was sitting his horse, looking as solid and serious as a judge. We asked him what he thought of the outlook? He said he didn't hardly know. We told him we were whipped, and whipped badly at that. The words were hardly out of our mouth when all the boys seemed to reach the same conclusion at once, and turned to run, every fellow on his own hook. It was about 200 yards through the lane already referred to to the timber. The officers were all commanding the men to halt, but as a rule, every time they would give the command halt, they would bury the rowels of their big spurs deep in their horses' sides. We all reached the end of the lane about the same time. The writer found one of his company, a long hungry fellow from Wise County, by the name of Pennington, here. He said: "Hello, Bob, let's stop and fight them." Of course, being his company commander, we said: "All right; fall in and form a line." We succeeded in getting about a dozen men in line parallel with the road, and when we came to examine we found that it was not Pennington's bravery or patriotism which had prompted him to make the stand, but that his horse had been killed, and he was riding a little black, thirteen-hands-high mule, without saddle or bridle. The remainder of our command went by like a gust of wind. Pretty soon our squad began leaving, one at a time. A young man by the name of Landrum was sitting his horse next to the writer, and as his flea-bitten gray mare lit into the road a bullet broke her neck. The writer's horse jumped clear over Landrum, and as we went over he called to us to let him ride behind us. We told him we could not spare the time. When our little squad dashed up behind the command they thought we were Federals. When the boys looked back at us their eyes, in contrast with their dirty faces, looked as white and snowy as dogwood blossoms in early spring. Some of them commenced crying, while others took to the woods. The writer saw at once that the wire edge was all knocked off them, and that our personal safety depended on a square run, so we quit the big road and took to the brush. The woods seemed to be full of "us," and we were making the brush pop like a drove of longhorn Texas cattle on a stampede.

After going about a mile we returned to the road and passed through a lane, and our command halted. While sitting there on our horses we noticed some of the boys craning their necks and poking their eyes down the lane like they saw something. Some one said: "Look, yonder they come now." At this the boys who had dismounted climbed into their saddles, and all eyes were "pinted" down the lane. We were just on the eve of breaking when Capt. Faulkner drew his pistol and threatened to shoot the first man that broke. He cursed like a Turk, and said if he had known that was the way Texans conducted themselves in battle he never would have come all the way from the State of New York to help them. Capt. Faulkner was only about twenty years of age, a fine specimen of young manhood, smart as a whip and brave almost to rashness.

He and one of his lieutenants, John Q. Daugherty, another brave and good man, with four privates remained in the neighborhood of the battle grounds over night and buried our dead the next morning, leaving a list of the names of the dead with a family near by, as well as placing marked headboards at their graves. Gov. Johnson removed the remains of his son and interred them in the family burying grounds near Johnson Station, Texas. Some years after the war ended and in a spirit of common fairness, it is but left for us to say, that Capt. Faulkner did more hard fighting, put his life in peril more times than any Confederate soldier from Texas, in proportion to the interest he had in a Southern Confederacy, as he did not own a dollar's worth of property, and had no blood kin south of Mason and Dixon line. But he fought his way up from a private soldier to a major's commission, and was wearing a five point gold star on his collar when the war ended.

His picture is at the beginning of this chapter, and many perhaps, who have not met the jolly captain will not recognize it, but all who have read their tickets while riding on the good Houston & Texas Central railroad in the last twenty years will recognize his peculiar sign-manual; and had some day-dreamer said to the writer thirty years ago, when we were waltzing around in Arkansas doing service for the good of the Confederacy, under orders, made authority by this rare signature, that in 1893 we would ride on a handsomely equipped steel track railway from Denton, Texas, to the great city of St. Louis, on a complimentary pass from him, as the chief of its passenger department, we would have moved to have had him restrained as a dangerous lunatic; but during all these years of phenomenal success, he never lost his balance, even if he did have an eye for a pretty woman and fine horses. We have devoted this much space to the friend of our young manhood and riper years as well, because he has a place in our heart of hearts, and that young men may learn from this object lesson that there is room at the top, on the roll of honor, and distinction in all legitimate undertakings, to be reached at the end of an honest, brave, persistent effort, under our free institutions.

But to return to our story. On the enemy seemed to be coming, raising a cloud of dust. Some one said, "There don't seem to be but one of them, and he is afoot." Bob Floyd, of Wise county, suggested that we fall back into the brush and "fire on him as he goes by," but it turned out to be our friend Landrum. He came up puffing like a steam engine, and we felt right smartly relieved.

As we rode along in the deep darkness that night, on our way back to Batesville, we had a fine opportunity for reflection and rumination, and we went a good ways out on the line of reaching the conclusion that few things in real war come up to the colored pictures in the books.

The following is the full text of Col. Sweet's report of the battle, as appeared in the Little Rock, Ark., Gazette.

HEADQUARTERS 15TH REG'T TEXAS CAVALRY,
    BATESVILLE, ARK., July 12, 1862.

*Capt. Hart, Ass't Adj't-Gen'l Brig.-Gen'l Rust:*

SIR—I have the honor to report the result of a scout by a portion of my command, consisting of one hundred and fifty-one men, on the 8th inst.

Learning about 10 o'clock, a. m., of that day, that a body of the enemy, said to be 258 strong, were coming down from the direction of Salem, in Fulton county en route for Jacksonport, via Sulphur Rock and Orient Ferry, on Black river, I immediately ordered a forward movement of a portion of my command, having it in view to take the lower road leading from Batesville to Jacksonport, and to intercept the enemy and cut him off from the ferry.

The command was very soon put in motion, and proceeded as rapidly as the excessive heat of the weather and the jaded condition of our horses would permit; but notwithstanding all my precautions and vigilance, before I had reached the place I had hoped to intercept him, he had made good his retreat to the ferry. Determined not to be completely foiled, I concluded to follow him and give him battle, though I knew I should have to fight a largely superior force to my own, in point of numbers. I believed I could come upon him so suddenly as to completely surprise him, and perhaps to effect a complete victory before he could fairly recover from the shock. To effect this, I made the following disposition of my forces: Capt. Thos. J. Johnson, my quartermaster, was assigned, at his own request, to the command of ten men, as an advance picket, to keep well in the advance until we should near the enemy, when all were to move nearly together. Next to Capt. Johnson, was placed Capt. A. Faulkner, of Troop G, in charge of the rifles and sharpshooters, and after these, the main body, led by myself.

Being anxious to make the fight before dark, we moved with all possible speed, and about half an hour before sunset, came upon what was supposed to be the enemy's pickets. Capt. Johnson captured one of them, the other escaped. It turned out, however, that the enemy had no pickets out, and that we were right on the main body. A charge was immediately ordered by the advance, and executed with telling effect. Capt. Faulkner followed with his command in a sweeping gallop, the main body moving close behind him. Unfortunately for us, we had to charge down a lane, and could only move four abreast; and before the main body could gain position, both our advance (including Capt. Faulkner's rifles) and the enemy became enveloped in such a cloud of dust and smoke from the fire of our guns, that for a few minutes, it was impossible to distinguish friend from foe. This was most fortunate for the enemy. He was thus given time to rally. I immediately galloped to the front to ascertain against what point to direct my column. I found that nearly all the enemy's force on the north side of the river (a considerable portion had previously crossed the river) was put to flight, except a few who had taken shelter behind some old buildings and trees, and some who had taken position under cover of a train of wagons which almost completely blocked up the road near the ferry. I ordered a charge for the purpose of driving these squads from their hiding places, whence they were deliberately firing upon our advance. By this time, that portion of the enemy on the opposite side of the river, having recovered from the panic, had formed in line of battle, and was pouring a galling fire on our entire line; a fire which was particularly severe on the advance of the main body which, under command of Capt. Sanders, had already been ordered up to the support of the rifles. Notwithstanding this severe fire, the first squadron came into position in fine order, and commenced delivering its fire to the enemy on the opposite side of the river, 200 yards distant. I soon found that this was too long a range for our shot-guns, and ordered a charge over the hill right down next to the river, where a large number of the enemy was secreted under a bluff close to the water's edge. This charge I attempted to lead in person; but as my command moved to the front it was thrown into some disorder by the rifles, who had gotten into confusion, and completely blocked up the passage. At the same time my horse was killed under me, and before order could be restored, the entire command had fallen back about 200 yards. I was still on foot, when Capt. Sherwood offered me a seat on his horse, behind him, which I accepted until we both came up with the command, where I obtained another horse, and endeavored to rally the men, but the enemy was now pouring a perfect shower of balls upon my broken and confused columns, and I soon found all attempts to reform under such a fire impracticable. I therefore ordered a retreat beyond the range of the enemy's guns, where, after some difficulty, I succeeded in restoring order and reforming. By this time I had learned from the prisoner captured that we had been fighting the whole, or nearly the whole, of the 5th Kansas regiment, and was satisfied also, from the reception we had met, that the odds of numbers against us was so great, and such the enemy's advantage of position, it would be imprudent to renew the attack, and hence continued the retreat.

Our loss in the engagement was seven men killed and seven wounded, 18 horses killed and four wounded, besides some others so slightly as not to be reported. Two of the men are badly wounded, but I believe all will recover. We brought off all our wounded, except private Jones, who was accidentally shot as we went down, and left at a house half a mile north of the battle ground.

It is impossible to obtain an accurate account of the enemy's loss, as he was left in possession of the field, and would not allow any citizen to visit the scene of the conflict until all his dead had been buried and his wounded carried off. Some of the men acknowledged to the citizens of Jacksonport a loss of twenty-five killed and a like number wounded. There were above forty horses without riders when the enemy passed through Jacksonport on the following morning. Besides, the night after the engagement, the enemy destroyed nearly all his train and camp and garrison equipage, and evidently left in haste. From these facts I am convinced that he considered himself roughly handled, and dreaded another attack.

Early on the morning after the engagement, I dispatched Capt. James E. Moore, with a flag of truce, to bury our dead; but he met Capt. Faulkner and Lieut. Dougherty, who had been ordered to fall back, with a rear guard and watch the movements of the enemy, returning from the field where he had been to bury the dead, after he found the enemy had left.

I mention with feelings of gratitude the gallant conduct of Capt. A. Faulkner, who had two horses shot under him, whilst rallying his men to the charge. Capt. V. P. Sanders and Capt. Thos. E. Sherwood also displayed signal coolness and bravery; as also did Lieuts. Dougherty and Banister, the last named being severely wounded in both arms — his right arm badly shattered by a minnie ball. Many of the privates exhibited great coolness and determination in the fight, and are deserving of special mention; but where all did so well, it would be invidious to distinguish. Let the gallant conduct of the brave bring the blush of shame when they remember it, to the cheeks of those who sneaked away without firing a gun.

It is with a sad heart that I have to report the loss of Capt. Thos. J. Johnson of my staff. He fell, shot through the head, whilst gallantly leading his brave little band in a most desperate charge. He was brave almost to a fault. I trust his country will do honor to his memory.

We captured two prisoners — one soldier and one teamster; also a blacksmith's forge with a complete set of tools, horse shoes, etc.

I regret, for the sake of humanity, to be compelled to report the barbarous conduct of the enemy in killing Private Jones, the wounded man left at the house on the road, as before stated. After my command had retired from the field a small party of the enemy's calvary came out on the road in the direction we had taken, and finding Jones, deliberately shot him in the head, although he had not been in the fight, and was wholly unable to make any resistance. Can such an enemy prosper? God forbid it. GEO. H. SWEET,
*Colonel Com'dg.*

M. SHELBY KENNARD, *Adjutant.*

Thirty years may be a long time, and a very great distance from the transaction, to set up a criticism, but the writer was a member of the Rifles, and living witnesses will testify that the only confusion in, and the blocking of the way as referred to by Col. Sweet, was caused by wounded men and horses, and the small space of ground we had to fight on.

## CHAPTER V.

ORDERED TO REPORT AT LITTLE ROCK — DISMOUNTED AND PUT INTO CAMP OF INSTRUCTION IN THE INFANTRY DRILL — MUSIC IN THE AIR — MOVED TO ARKANSAS POST.

The writer and little squad arrived at Batesville about daylight, all fully impressed with the idea that there was something to do beyond finding and catching up with the Yankee soldier.

We crossed the river and went to our former camp, spread our pallet under a great sugar tree, and napped until about 12 o'clock. The boys were coming in, one, two, three in a "gang" all day, and as we had been blessed with the happy, sunshiny, God-given faculty of taking in all the ridiculous phases of the life of a soldier, we called all the boys around us and had them relate their impressions, experiences, and how they had seen the battle. We had fun enough that afternoon and laughed enough to satisfy the fun-loving side of any ordinary grown man a whole life time. Some of them said the Yankees had guns as long as fence rails; some said the balls they shot at us were as long as yard sticks.

After a few days we were ordered to report at Little Rock. Here the 14th, 15th, 16th, 17th and 18th Texas cavalry were dismounted and made into infantry regiments, and put into a brigade with the 10th Texas infantry, commanded by Col. Allison Nelson, of Waco, Texas. Col. Nelson was afterwards made a Brigadier-General C. S. A., and Lieutenant Colonel R. Q. Mills was elected Colonel of the regiment. We were put into a camp of instruction near some fine springs, a few miles from a little city called Austin. Here we were first introduced to the real life of a soldier, and put through a routine of duty each day peculiar to a regular army. Brigadier-General Nelson was put in command of the Division, and the duty of disciplining the brigade devolved on Col. George H. Sweet. Col. Sweet was an Ulster county, New York, man, well educated, a fine specimen of American manhood, and had seen some service in the war between the United

States and Mexico, having marched with Scott to the City of Mexico, as well as having served through one campaign in Virginia, as a private in Capt. Ed Cunningham's company, in the early days of the war. He had a hard time breaking five thousand wild Texans into the infantry harness. Fact is, we were all mad because we had been dismounted, having had our hearts set on doing our soldiering on horseback, and the boys very unjustly charged all this misfortune and hard camp duty, drilling, strict guard duty, etc., to Col. Sweet. Some of the men from the 18th regiment went to his headquarters one night and shaved the mane and tail of his fine charger, Bay Bob, and after that whenever the Colonel would come in sight of the command the boys would commence hallooing "Whoa, Bob," at the top of their voices. This annoyed the Colonel very much, as he was a proud, vain and very sensitive man.

Some time during the month of October our command was marched to Clarendon, on White river, some sixty miles from our camp. Just what this march was made for we did not know at the time and have not learned since, as we neither saw nor heard of any enemy in all those regions. It rained on us one whole day as we crossed the Grand Prairie. After a few days we returned to our old camp, where the same routine of drilling, guard mount, Sunday parade and inspection was gone through with.

About this time Brig.-Gen. Nelson took sick and died. Brig.-Gen. A. Deshler was put over us. He had resigned a captain's commission in the United States army, was a graduate of West Point, a thorough gentleman and every inch a soldier. We all fell right in with him, and the longer we were with him and under his command the better we liked him. His soul quit this mortal coil in the great battle of Chickamauga.

About the 15th of December our command was marched to Little Rock and there put on boats and shipped to Arkansas Post. The river was very low, and we were some four or five days making the trip. Most of the time we were out our boats were hung up on sand bars, and about half the boys would wade out and forage through the country. We spent Christmas at the Post. During Christmas week our old boss, Mr. Daniel Howell, the merchant for whom the writer was clerking when the war commenced, made us a visit, driving all the way from Decatur, Texas, to Arkansas Post in a two-horse carry-all. His good wife had prepared us a lot of warm underclothing, overshirts, socks, etc., a trunk full, which he brought to us; but we lost them all in the battle which occurred a few days later. While here Mr. Howell offered to buy the writer a sheep ranch or a drug store, or go in with him in running the blockade and getting up a trade with Mexico, if he would quit the army, but we could not "see it." We had not got glory enough yet, but we learned later on that we had acted the fool in not accepting one of his propositions. But you cannot put an old man's head on a young man's shoulders, and there is no use trying it.

About January 8th, 1863, the writer was laid up with the flux and fever. Our quarters were only a few yards from the graveyard, we were very low, came very near handing in our checks, and the salutes they would fire over the graves of soldiers as they buried them each day was not calculated to brace one up much.

## CHAPTER VI.

### BATTLE OF ARKANSAS POST.

No one knows as much about the great difference between the written and unwritten history of the great war as does the soldier and the officers of the line, because of the hard experiences, the pathetic scenes, the never dying attachments formed under circumstances that tried men's weak points and developed all the good in human nature, to say nothing of the fun we had in taking in from day to day all the ridiculous phases in a great army of volunteers thrown together from all the States, of every grade of intelligence, from the cow boy on the frontier, the farmer boy from the rural districts, the clerk from the counter, the merchant from his ledger, the lawyer from his books, the preacher from his pulpit, the mechanic from his jack plane, and all, all, from the civil walks of life and as full of fight as were the legions that followed Cæsar and Napoleon. But enough of this, we have already spread all over the country and haven't said a word about what we picked up our tablet and faber to write. So here is at it.

In the early winter of 1862 there were three thousand of us rebels at a place on the Arkansaw river, known as Arkansaw Post, and this little army was armed with shot-guns in the main, while a few regiments had the old buck and ball musket, and a few companies were armed with Enfield rifles. About the first of January, 1863, Gen. Sherman with an army of forty thousand men, equipped with all the conveniences and death-dealing appliances of modern warfare, went down to and bucked up against Vicksburg and was repulsed with great loss. While he was yet mad, somebody told him that Tom Churchill, a little bit of a spike-tail, snaffle-bit dude of an Arkansaw Brigadier-General, was up there on the Arkansaw with a small outfit of rebels, and that he had better drive up that way and take them in. We were only about one hundred miles up the river, and there was hardly room for Sherman's fleet of transports and "wash-pot throwing" gunboats: anyway he managed to get there, and after about two days maneuvering and feeling his way, he finally strung out his forty thousand around our three thousand, his lines extending from the river below to the river above, with his gunboats in our rear. During the night of the 10th of January, 1863, his gunboats threw shells as big as wash-pots with tails of fire as long as a clothes line all over the river bottom and the explosions of them was so deafening and terrific that we would have gladly exchanged for keen claps of thunder. All this while we were not lying flat on the ground, but were as busy as busy could be in throwing up earthworks, each man working fully impressed with the opinion that every shovel of dirt he piled in his front might save his hide from being perforated by a bullet on the morrow. The morning of the 11th came bright, cold, calm, crispy. In our front was a prairie and open woodland, as level as the plains of Texas, and it was covered as thick with blue coats as ever you saw blackbirds on an oat stack in midwinter, getting things in shape to walk our logs. About eleven o'clock, here they came. Our line of rebels craned their necks over our line of earthworks, doubtless realizing the fact that we had found what we had been looking for — an opportunity to whip ten to one. On they came in magnificent style, as regular as one blue wave follows another on the bosom of old ocean's howling wastes. When the front line was within about eighty yards of our works, our boys raised up and gave what was called a rebel yell, but it did not sound anything like such as we gave when we were on the march and some pretty Southern woman would shake a white rag at us, but it sounded weak and had a hollow, graveyard twang to it. Our shot-guns and buck got in their work and the enemy went down like grain before the mower, except those who had a good pair of legs and turned to account the good running grounds in their rear; but they formed and reformed, and bucked at us ever so many times during the day with the same results. By 4 o'clock in the evening all our artillery horses had been killed, rendering our field pieces as voiceless as the tomb of Saul, our big gun in the fort, "Lady Davis," had been shot into just below her corset by one of the big gunboats and put the silence of death on that end of our line. The gunboats in our rear boomed up smoke in great dark thunder-heads of inky blackness, hiding the face of the sun, giving everything as ghastly and weird appearance as if the caps from an hundred purgatories had been lifted. To add to this heart-sinking situation not a gun was being fired by either side, the sun seemed to have run its golden chariot into the top of a big cottonwood tree and we were ready to believe that the Yankees had a Joshua in their camps. This dreadful suspense was relieved when we looked to the right and saw a little white rag fixed in the end of a ramrod and fluttering in the breeze. They said it was raised through mistake, but it is too late to discuss that matter now. The Yankees in front of us rose up as if by magic and were soon marched up to our lines. They seemed to be in excellent humor, while our boys, as a rule, looked pretty sullen when ordered to stack their arms.

Our earthworks lacked some two or three hundred yards of reaching the creek or bayou on our left. Lieut. Ira Long, commanding Company G, was ordered to take his company, and deploy it as skirmishers and guard the space in the timber between our left and the creek, hence theirs was an open field fight all day, and notwithstanding the Federal right pressed them, they held their ground, and when they discovered what was going on to the right — the white flag and other signs that the day was lost — Lieut. Long, Sgt. Dan McGary, and many others made good their escape by swimming the creek and a lake, and made their way back to Texas, and afterwards did good service under Kirby Smith, in the Trans-Mississippi Department.

## CHAPTER VII.

THE FEDERALS ISSUE LOTS OF RATIONS, PUT OUR OUTFIT ON BOATS AND LIGHT OUT FOR THE NORTH.

After the surrender we were marched off down to the river. A strong guard was stationed around us and big rations of Lincoln coffee, hard tack and bacon was issued to us, and before dark came, several big Union Generals rode around outside the guard lines, looking through their spectacles, and over them too, in an effort to size up the build of such a small body of men who had held such a great army at bay so long.

After stowing a big share of the rations away in a safe place, the Yankee boys bantered us for a singing match. Curg Smith, of Capt. Faulkner's Denton County company, accepted the challenge, and a goodly number of the Yankees formed a line on the outside and rendered the Star Spangled Banner with a hearty gusto, and by the time the last note had floated away on the cool evening wind, Curg and his crowd sailed into "The Girl I Left Behind Me," and for the time Federals and Confederates were all one, a general shout going up from everybody. Next the Federals put up "Hail Columbia, Happy Land," and the thoughtful man discerned a seriousness in the rebels while this was being rendered, that spoke more than is written in the book. But we were not knocked out by a large majority. We sailed into "Happy Land of Canaan." This was new to the Federals and they seemed to enjoy it. "Dixie" and the "Bonnie Blue Flag" were sung, and the meed of victory was awarded the rebels, which of course was polite, we being their guests.

On the morning we were marched aboard transports for a trip, and God only knew where, as far as we were concerned. The writer and about seventeen hundred others were put on a great big old wheezy, crazy boat called the Nebraska. After on board, the captain arranged to have the field staff and officers of the line take their meals in the cabin and occupy state rooms like regular passengers, and the non-commissioned officers and privates to occupy the hold, boiler and hurricane decks. His intentions were doubtless good, but his judgment was grievously at fault. The first dinner he set knocked all his well laid plans awry. The men and officers as a rule were dressed alike, and before the meal was over he cursed like a good sailor, and said he didn't know that every man in the outlay was an officer, or he certainly would not have undertaken the job of feeding and bedding them in the cabin. We thought we had a dead sinch on him, but this was the first and only meal he set. We lay there all day and when old Sol had rode down the hill "away yonder" the other side of home and Texas, and thick darkness had quiet possession of the dark river bottoms, and the little stars above us looked like cat eyes up a dark alley, and no sound save the "gourd sawing" of the sound-sleeping rebel, the thorough bass of the bull-frog as he waded down right through the middle of the music of the spheres, and the sentinel at his post as he cried the hour of the night and "all is well!"— under these conditions several of the boys slid over the gunwales of the boat and made their escape. Joe Robinson from Denton County made the attempt and was either drowned or shot, as we found his hat the next morning. The hat was identified by having under its inside sweatband a note the writer had sent him some days before the battle. Early on the morning of the 13th everything was in ship-shape for the Sam Gaty, John J. Roe and Nebraska, the boats which we were on, to sail. When we awoke on the morning of the 14th we were floating on the bosom of the Father of Waters, and a blinding snow-storm was getting in its work. By this time the boys had pretty well all become located. Some were in the hold of the vessel; and for darkness, dampness and grown folk rats, it won the cake. Messes were tucked away in every nook and corner. Alec Williams, Hugh McKenzie, Lieut. Bill Brown and the others of their mess compromised with the firemen and pitched their quarters in front of the fire-box, while some spread their bedding on the brick covering of the big boilers and some made their headquarters on the hurricane deck and managed to stand off the "shrewd and biting" north wind by taking it by turns in standing close to the great chimneys of the boat.

The floor of the cabin was set aside as the

hospital. The whole outfit was thinly clad, all their clothing, except what they had on when captured, having been appropriated or destroyed by the enemy, and having just come out of warm, cosy, winter quarters and moving to the north, that dreadful disease, pneumonia, found a rich harvest, and in a very few days the cabin floor was lined from one end to the other with sick men, two rows of them with their heads toward the center and their feet toward the state room doors. The big stove in the ladies' cabin was kept full of coal and the hot, burning fever of the sick made the cabin too warm for a well man, and the sharp, biting wind on the outside was more than we could stand. We would go on the outside and slash around until the cold would drive us in, and when we would open the door, a volume of hot air, laden with a stench, would strike us in the face strong enough to hang your hat on.

After awhile the spires, domes and minarets of Memphis, Tenn., hove in sight and the hearts of the boys bounded with hope and joy because the Yankees had told us we would be paroled there. Guess they told us this lie to keep us from getting away while on the Arkansas side.

The boats rounded to and to our astonishment everything was moving along in Memphis as if there was no trouble going on down in Dixie. The stores so far as we could judge were full and people seemed as busy trading and trafficking as if nothing had happened. We looked, watched and waited for the man to come along with the paroles, but "nary" parole did we see.

The boats took on a supply of coal, bacon, crackers, coffee and some more sugar, and pulled out up the river, and our hearts sank within us.

## CHAPTER VIII.

TRIP UP THE GREAT RIVER TO ST. LOUIS — SICK MEN ON BOARD — STOPPING TO BURY THE DEAD — ONE OF OUR MEN SHOT TO DEATH BY THE GUARD AT BELMONT, MO. — ARRIVED AT COLUMBUS, OHIO.

We were several days out before reaching St. Louis, and while our surroundings were not at all inviting and all hands stood ready to make any sort of change that presented, yet there was something going on all the time, which had a decided tendency to relieve the dull monotony and turn on a whole lot of cheery sunshine. One bright crispy morning, while we were sailing somewhere above Columbus, Kentucky, our big boat took on some sort of a crazy fit. The pilot seemed to be working his wheel all right, and the captain was doing his best swearing, but it all did no good, the old boat flopped up against the bank of the river sidewise like a hog goes to war. The bank was quite perpendicular with deep water right up to it and was just as high as the hurricane deck and as soon as the boat struck the bank the boys on the hurricane deck jumped off like sheep out of a dry lot over the bars into pastures green. The guard being stationed inside the railing around the cabin, they could not see what was going on. Several of the boys made their escape. The captain was a tall, handsome, blue-eyed man, and many Texans are to-day carrying around with them recollections of him in their heart of hearts. He was either a rebel at heart, or he had a heart full of sympathy for suffering humanity, anyway, he made it a point to throw all the good things he could in our way. The boat rounded to land every day or so to bury the dead. One instance, we clearly remember, there were two negro men on our boat. One was the body servant of Col. John T. Coit, of the 18th Texas regiment, and the other was the servant of some one else. Anyhow, the Federals showed them some extra attention by spreading out some boards over the boilers for a sleeping-place for them. One good morning one of the bucks "waked up dead," but seeing the dead and dying was no uncommon thing and it did not attract much attention. Soldiers, as a rule, get to be hardshell Baptists or fatalists and go into whatever falls to their lot, as being a part of that only which is to come to pass, according to the arrangements made by a higher power.

At, or near, the battlefield of Belmont, Mo., our boat landed for fuel, and during the time the hands were getting it on board, some half-dozen very pretty young ladies came down to the shore and threw snow-balls to the boys. When the boat was just backing out, a very handsome man, a private in some one of the Texas regiments, remarked that he had rather die than remain a prisoner, and he leaped from the hurricane deck to the bank and fell, and by the time he arose to his feet six or eight of the guard fired on him. He sank down at once. The young ladies on the bank rushed to him and held him up, one being on each side. As the boat steamed off we could see him, his head fell forward, and they gently laid him down on the snow. His spirit had gone where wars and rumors of wars never come.

As we sailed by a town in Missouri, called Cape Girardeau, the boys enjoyed the didos cut by the negro population (in fact negroes seemed to be about the only population in the town). When they discovered we were rebel prisoners their joy seemed to know no bounds. A limber jack is a tame specimen of a gyrator as compared to the shines cut by bucks, boys and wenches on the shore. They would get down on their hands and knees and paw snow like the bulls of Bashan going to war.

One instance of what cheek and nerve can do for a man, and we will pass along. Col. Majors, of Texas, was a tall, handsome fellow, and had by some means come into possession of a Yankee hat, coat and pants. He had his boots blacked, and had a nice shirt and collar, and while our boat was tied up at Cairo, Col. Majors and a lot of other Confederate officers were standing on the hurricane deck. He said: "Right here is my time and place to get away." We all laughed at the idea. The wharf was crowded with Yankee troops and the sidewalks with citizens. He walked right down to the gang plank, saluted the guard and the guard returned the salute and made room for him to pass out. We stood and watched him until he went out of sight up Main street. He made his escape and his way back to Texas.

After about twelve days of the filthiest and most disagreeable living we ever struck in all our history, we came in sight of the city of Louis XIV, St. Louis. While here Capt. Bill Shannon, of Parker County, Texas, played Col. Majors' trick on them, but after three or four days in the city the secret detectives shadowed him and took him in out of the wet. While here we were guarded by a regiment of home guard gray beards. They looked to be on an average about 75 years of age, and their long gray beards, as a rule, extended down to their belts. They were in full Federal uniform and were the most dignified body of men we have ever seen. Our boys poked all sorts of good humor at them, but not a word would they say, and not a muscle on their face could we cause to move. Here the trading and trafficking proclivities of the Yankee showed up. The hucksters filled the boat, and as we rebels had nothing but old issue "Confederic" money, the first thing to be done was to fix a fair discount on our kind of money. The writer swapped a twenty dollar bill for four one-dollar greenback bills, and the first thing he invested in was a hunk of limburger cheese about as big as a dinner bucket, and of great value because of its age, and there "were millions in it." (This chunk of cheese will come in later on.)

After a day or so dickering as to what they would do with us, a conclusion was reached that the dividing line between the sheep and the goats be drawn, and the sheep be sent to Camp Douglas, Chicago, and the goats to Camp Chase, Columbus, Ohio, or in other words, the non-commissioned officers and privates be sent to the former place and the field staff and officers of the line to the latter. There were, somewhere in the neighborhood of three hundred commissioned officers in the layout. We were shipped to Cincinnati in common stock cars that had been used for shipping cattle, and the filth on the floors was shoe-mouth deep, and we had our choice of standing up and sleeping like horses, or of laying down and sleeping like hogs in this filth. Nature gave away after awhile and we spread our blankets as best we could in the darkness and laid down. The first night was bitter cold. A Lieutenant Rodgers, from Texas, froze to death. At Cincinnati we changed cars, and the change was a welcome one, because they put us into nice passenger coaches, nicely heated. The most disagreeable thing we had to contend with on the way to Columbus, was the disposition of the guards in our coach to sing. The only song they seemed to know or care anything about was, " We will hang Jeff Davis on a sour apple tree," etc. At Dayton, Ohio, the writer handed a Federal soldier 80 cents to buy mince pies. He returned in a short time with a stack of them as high as a cedar churn and about the size of a saucer. We felt rich beyond computation. And oh, how deliciously good they tasted. We sat there with them on our lap, one disappearing at a time, along with the cheese before referred to. After awhile we felt " kinder" full, our head began to swim, big drops of sweat oozed out, our neck veins swelled and throbbed and our over-loaded stomach seemed to want to turn over and rest on the other side. We raised the window for some fresh air and as the air came in, we stuck our head out, and with an ordinary bow of our back and swell in our Confederate neck, the tail end of the pies and cheese came forth, and as the train moved the cheese and pies came out of our mouth like a rope of dough and did not break until the first pie we ate was all gone. We washed out our mouth, wiped the tears from our eyes and cheeks, felt as cool as a cucumber and was as hungry as ever. At low twelve we arrived at Columbus.

## CHAPTER IX.

LUNCHED BY MRS. A. G. THURMAN — MARCH TO CAMP CHASE — SEARCHED, REGISTERED AND TURNED INTO PRISON WITH AS MUCH BUSINESS COOLNESS AS A TEXAS COWMAN MARKS BRANDS AND TURNS A CALF LOOSE ON THE PRAIRIE.

Getting us off the cars was the work of only a few minutes, and we were formed into two ranks on a broad street in front of a large hotel. The ground was frozen stiff and the north wind bit "shrewdly," the skies were as clear as a bell, and the bright fires in the hotel, and well-dressed people moving around was quite in contrast with the condition of the 300 rebel officers standing out and shivering in the cold. During the time that all the red tape fixing up peculiar to the military, several ladies came down our line with baskets filled with cakes, pies, fried chicken, roast beef, etc., — in fact it was as nicely fixed up as if it had been intended for a Sunday school picnic. They issued it out to us like sisters of charity with neither words of condemnation or approval. We surmised at the time that some great and good-hearted woman was the power back of all this, and it afterwards came to light that the wife of Allen G. Thurman did all this for us, and it was used against him when he ran for vice-president on the ticket with Mr. Cleveland.

About 1 o'clock a. m. we were ordered into line and moved out on the national pike. We reached Camp Chase, which was about 4 miles out from the city, about 3:30 o'clock a. m., and in this short time the heavens became overcast with heavy, dark, threatening clouds, and by the time the head of the column reached the prison door a blinding snow storm set in.

The work of relieving us of everything offensive and defensive before turning us loose on the inside was went at in a thorough, systematic manner. We were let into a kind of ante room, one at a time. After giving our name, rank, regiment and State, a big burly Federal soldier went through our pockets like an expert. He would then overhaul us from the crown of our heads to the soles of our feet, in order to be sure that we had no gunboats, torpedoes, shot-guns, or mountain howitzers about our old clothes. After all this, which was gone through with so quick and with such familiar handling of one's person and effects that we felt in a kind of dazed, wonder-what-comes-next condition, he would grab us by the point of our shoulder and shove us through another door where about the same proceedings were had. Through with this and we were shoved through the door inside of the great high walls of the prison, and we felt about as blank and as much dazed as a yearling looks to be after having been marked, branded, his tail cut off and then thrown over the fence to rustle for itself.

By this time the snow was coming down in full-grown flakes. We looked up at the sentinels on the walls as they paced their beat with their great coats and other warm clothing protecting them from the cold.

Down through the center of the inclosure were two rows of buildings, each about 300x15 feet with street between them. These were cut up into rooms about 12x15, each being furnished with a small cooking stove, cooking utensils and plenty of blankets. The bunks were arranged something like the shelving in a store with room for two. We were not long in finding a vacant room, when we kindled a fire in the stove, toasted some of our cheese, fried some of our mince pies and lunched before going to bed. After lunch we went about the matter of getting off to bed, and upon investigation we found that those who had been in there before us, had left a big lot of hungry "gray backs," who were holding under the ancient and strong law of peaceable possession. A compromise was made on the basis that we furnish board and the "gray backs" the bedding. We were not long straightening out the big government blankets, and were very soon sleeping as sweetly and soundly in the arms of morpheus as if we had never made any trouble with the so-called "best government the world ever saw." When we awoke the next morning the writer was sick all the way through, up and down; the mixture of mince pies and cheese had again gone to war, and we turned them out where they could fight in an open field. We have never had anything like a "honing" for pies and cheese since.

The day was bright and cold as it can be

only in that hard, cold climate, and during the day the dickering was all done as to forming messes, and the regular issuing of rations began, which as a rule consisted of cornmeal, baker's bread, beef, pickle pork, navy beans, cabbage, carrots, onions, sugar and coffee. Of course the items given above were not all issued at the same time, but we give the above as a sample of the way the rations run. While at Camp Chase we were well fed. The confinement and having to go to bed at 9 o'clock or sit up in the dark, and bounce out of bed at daylight and answer to roll-call were some of the disagreeable things we had to endure. The policy of the authorities was to put twenty in each mess. However, the messes ranged from 13 to 20 and taking it for granted that the reader will accept a description of the daily walk and godly conversation of the writer's mess as a sample of the whole, we pass along.

In three or four days we were moved from prison No. 1 into No. 2, and in our new quarters we got down to housekeeping. We divided out into reliefs of two to do the cooking. We remember the following of our messmates: Capt. F. J. Barrett; Lieut. W. C. Burris of Texas,

Lieut. Wm. Cook, Texas; Capt. James Selkirk, Matagorda, Texas,— he was originally from Albany, New York; Maj. D. C. Douglas, 14th Tennessee Cavalry; Lieut. Furguson of Kentucky, —— Johnson, of Virginia. We have their names stowed away so far back in our memory now that we cannot call them all up. Capt. Selkirk's relatives living in York State, he was supplied with plenty of money. He was very liberal with his means, a perfect gentleman and as brave a Gen. Forrest. Maj. Douglas was a prince of good fellows. He loved to play seven-up, tell good stories and read Shakespeare. Lieut. Ferguson's folks over in Kentucky sent him several boxes of nice provisions and he always made them the common stock of the mess. The following was each day's routine, as a rule:—

Six o'clock a. m., roll call; next, breakfast; next, police quarters. By this time the morning papers were in. We were not permitted to read any but those that gave a favorable coloring to the Northern side of everything going on in Dixie.

Each mess was a regular workshop, putting in all their time in making rings out of overcoat buttons. We had full sets of jewelers' tools. When the weather was not too inclement we put in lots of time playing ball and foot racing. Capt. Sut Harris, of Tennessee, was the fleetest of all. At night we would sit around the stove in the dark and plot how to get out. We soon had prison No. 2 a net work of tunnels, but when some of our own folks did not sell us for their own personal freedom the authorities had spies in with us who would give us away before many could escape. All tools that we borrowed from the sutler during the day, such as hoes, shovels, hatchets, axes, etc., had to be returned the same day, and if any were held out, the rations of the mess holding them were cut off until the tools were returned.

We had two Methodist preachers with us, Rev. Gillespie, Colonel of the 24th Texas, and Rev. Wilks, Colonel of the 25th Texas. They would preach for us on Sunday when not hushed up by the officer of the day. We remember one nice, bright Sunday morning we were all on the ground in rows like chickens on a bean pole, and the Rev. Gillespie was dishing us out some good gospel from a text, where some lecherous, broken down king was making war on some one who was leading a rebellion against him. Col. Gillespie was lifting the king's scalp in an artistic manner, and the lines of comparison he was running seemed to point in the direction of Washington City. We were drinking it down like it was good medicine. The Federal officer soon got enough of it and ordered us to disband and go to our quarters. We did not question his authority but put on a waterbury movement at once.

## CHAPTER X.

ANDY JOHNSON, GOV. OF TENNESSEE, GOV. BRIGHT, OF INDIANA, AND GOV. TODD, OF OHIO, VISIT OUR PRISON — BIG CROWD OUT FROM COLUMBUS AND ENJOY SEEING US STRIPPED AS WE COME OUT OF PRISON — ELEVEN SHIRTS SKINNED OFF OF LIEUT. COOK BY SERG. EVANS.

During the time that we were in prison No. 2, Col. A. B. Norton, of Dallas, Texas, called to see us several times. Being an original Union man, he had gone north early in the war. He took with him his love for Texas and Texans, and the many little offices of kindness he did for us while in prison will never be forgotten until all the ex-Confederate prisoners who endured the hardships of prison life at Camp Chase shall have crossed over the river and "rest under the shade of the trees" to answer to roll-call with Lee, Johnston, Bragg, Hood, Grant, Meade, Hancock, and the long unnumbered list of soldiers brave, who quit this life in prison, hospital, or went up from amidst the smoke and din of the battle of Chickamauga, Corinth, Chattanooga, Atlanta, Kensaw Mountain, Murfreesborough, Franklin and Richmond.

While we were yet in No. 2 Andrew Johnson, military governor of Tennessee, Gov. Todd, of Ohio, and Bright, of Indiana, called on us. They were three fat, sleek, elegantly dressed governors, and had called ostensibly to see the boys, but really to see Gen. Churchhill, whose mess was just across the street from that of the writer's. They sounded the alarm at Gen. Churchhill's door and sent in their cards by Capt. Webber, post commandant, and during the time the general was dickering over the matter of receiving the governors, quite a crowd of rebel lieutenants, captains and colonels collected around them, and when Capt. Webber reported that the rebel general refused to see them, we all cheered. Andy Johnson turned around and gave us a look of contempt and withering scorn that would have made ordinary mortals quake in their boots. With our mind's eye we can see him to-day.

Every few days the monotony of our surroundings would be relieved by a new invoice of prisoners from the South, and then we would be able to get the truth as to how things were going on down in Dixie. We would visit from mess to mess and fill up on grapevine telegrams. Some messes seemed to have gone into politics and the discussions were lively and rasping at times. Col. R. Q. Mills' mess was one of this kind.

Col. John T. Coit's mess was a regular den of theological gladiators, the Colonel was a strict Presbyterian, a finished scholar, and a perfect gentlemen. Capt. S. G. Snead of Austin, Texas, had been educated for a Catholic priest, and was a ready debater. Capt. M. D. Marion of Athens, Texas, was a Christian, "so-called Campbellite," and three men of more incongruous religious opinions could not have been thrown together. We have spent many pleasant hours listening to their discussions, and then pass on to the political mess of Col. Mills, and from there into the literary mess of Gen. Deshler.

The officers of the 16th Texas, as a rule, messed together, and they would sing Methodist campmeeting songs, and especially when some of the officers of Col. Portwood's Arkansaw regiment would join in with them. Some messes were headquarters for chess, and others had checkers down to a science.

About the first of April we were all moved into prison No. 3, and by this time we had gotten everything in shape for housekeeping, and everything moving along as usual, when one day about high twelve the fog horn voice of Sergeant Evans called us all to fall in line with our traps packed ready for moving, and then commenced the rushing here and there, all hands packing up and putting together their accumulation of shirts, blankets, tools for making rings, pipes, etc. In a word, everything we thought we could get away with that would be of service when we got home to Dixie. The writer had a whole outfit of jeweler's tools hid away in a loaf of bread. Friends in the north had sent us lots of nice clothing and some of the boys put on as many as thirteen shirts, while others of us had blankets enough, rolled and tied up, to supply a company of rebels, little thinking that "the best laid plans of mice and men aft gang aglee." We were marched in column of two up to the big gate, through which we passed to the outside world. Commencing at the head of the list A, we were let out one at a time. This sort of proceedings caused us to suspicion that we were going to be put through some trying ordeal, and the whooping, yelling and immoderate laughing of a great crowd on the outside was conclusive proof that somebody was having great gobs of fun at somebody's expense. The name of the writer came pretty early on the list, and he stole a peep through the crack in the gate to see what the cutting up on the outside was about. The city of Columbus seemed to have sent all of its fun-loving old men, young men, boys, pretty girls, old maids and fast married women out to have some fun at our expense. Of course the two generals, Churchhill and Deshler and their personal staffs were let out first. They robbed Gen. Deshler of an overcoat he had paid his own money for. He was very indignant. Lieut. Bill Brown, of Denton County, had on ten shirts. Lieut. Blair, of Belton, had a pistol. A spy by the name of Alder, a Hungarian, messed with him, gained his confidence and gave him away. Lieut. Chitwood, of Johnson County, had on ten shirts. The first one of the C's was Lieut. Wm. Cook, of Wise County. Cook was a sort of sad-eyed Confederate, and was a great lover of fine,

"LIKE WORKING A PUMP-HANDLE."

all-wool, yard-wide shirts. The big sergeant grabbed him as he walked out and remarked, so that the great crowd could hear him: "Aren't you rather too broad across the shoulders, and too large across the corset for that pair of legs you are marchin' on?" Cook was like a lamb being lead to the slaughter, "he opened not his mouth." The sergeant was in his glory. He pulled open the bosom of Cook's shirts, and then commenced the work of taking them off. He would lift the shirt in front and bend him over like working a pump-handle and peel off a shirt over his head like an Indiana farmer skinning a rabbit. As he would skin them off the elegantly dressed crowd of females and "hemales" would laugh and yell with excruciating delight. The writer came next. His investment was in fine big U. S. blankets, he having weakened on the kit of tools before referred to, and left them on the inside, and when he put his hands on us to examine for shirts and things, he found nothing. His keen eye, however, spied our roll of blankets and he cut the nice, new leather straps we had them bound with, tossed all we had into the pile except our own old home-made Confederate blanket, gave us a shove with the command to "git," and the crowd yelled. Capt.

Bob Hopkins, of Denton County, had enough blankets to supply his company with. By the time the last man was out the pile of shirts, blankets and things loomed up like a haystack in a fog. In saying good-by to Camp Chase, we will remark that we were guarded by home troops, and they watched us like we were cut-throats and robbers.

On the way down to the city of Columbus, we saw Prentice, of the Louisville Courier Journal, standing by the way. He looked serious and careworn. His son Clarence was with us — a handsome, dashing fellow. He was afterwards killed in battle.

At Columbus we were put on board very nice passenger coaches and pulled out, may be so for Dixie and may be so for somewhere else, and it was for somewhere else.

Late Saturday evening we passed through Pittsburg, Pa., and from the smoke and great seething hot furnaces, and hard, dirty looking people, we were inclined to the opinion that his satanic majesty had leased one corner of the earth and was doing a land office business. This opinion was not entirely removed when we came in contact with the people. We changed cars here and during the time we were making the change the Pennsylvania-stay-at-home rebellion crushers sailed into us pretty rough with their fiery tongues, having a great deal to say about our being rebels and threatening Lee with fighting Joe Hooker.

From here we went in the direction of Philadelphia instead of towards Dixie, and our hearts sank within us. We knew as little about where we were going as if we had been the same number of cattle; but such is the life of a soldier.

## CHAPTER XI.

FROM PITTSBURG TO FORT DELAWARE — PASS THROUGH PHILADELPHIA ON SUNDAY EVENING — THE PRESENCE OF THREE HUNDRED REBEL OFFICIALS PUT SOME OF THE QUAKERS IN BAD HUMOR — A NARROW ESCAPE FROM BEING MOBBED.

As our train had no right of way and run on such time as no other train on the great road needed, we were smartly delayed. Anyway Sunday morning found us somewhere in the Alleghanies between Pittsburg and Harrisburg, climbing around the mountains, crossing rivers and heading deep canyons. The road made such sharp curves it seemed at times that the engineer and the conductor in the caboose could exchange "chaws" of tobacco. Of course the people all along the line knew that we were coming, and all hands turned out to see what sort of looking specimen of the "genus homo" a rebel was, and the comments after sizing us up was sometimes complimentary and sometimes pretty hard to endure. We had some friends even in Pennsylvania, for at Harrisburg some good soul dumped a bushel of oyster crackers on the floor of our car. About four o'clock in the afternoon we entered the historic and classic precincts of the Schuylkill river and as it was Sunday the whole of the population of the great city of Philadelphia seemed to have on their best "toggery" and turned out to see us, big, little, old and young, elegant gentlemen, thugs, thieves and roughs, ladies and wenches, fools, fops, dudes and dudines. The train moved just fast enough for the seething mass of gathering humanity to keep up with it in a clever walk, and it was all the guard could do to keep them from boarding the train and attacking us. We thought then and have not changed our opinion since, that the authorities had planned to have us mobbed. If not why were we put at the mercy of so many drunk and excited people. Many of them seemed to be wild and livid with rage. They would whip us in the face with miniature flags and men and women would scream like wild cats: "Hurrah for the union!" An Irish woman picked out

Nick Darnell of Dallas as the man who had killed her son, and it required an effort to keep her from getting on board the train and crawling Nick's hump. Our train, as well as we could tell, passed through the north or bay end of the city, and just as far as we could see up the broad, straight streets of the great old city, we could see people coming in a long run. Fact is, there seemed to be more able-bodied men in the city of Philadelphia than we had in all the armies of the Confederate States. As the train glided into a big depot, an iron gate was shut and the excited crowd surged against it like so many cattle. This was the first sure indication that our guards were alarmed as to their own as well as our safety. We were hurried out the other end of the depot and on board a steamer, where we felt pretty safe and could draw a long breath. The writer, along with some others, went on the hurricane deck, and after looking at the shipping in the bay turned to get a good view of the city. Here was a sight that baffles description. We never before nor since have seen such a mass of human beings. We felt well out of danger and full of fun, and yelled at the top of our voice: "Hurrah for Jeff Davis and the Southern Confederacy!" In an instant we were sorry we had done it, for it brought forth a groan mingled with hisses from that seething mass of infuriated Yankees that made each particular hair on our head stand up like the quills on the back of the fretted porcupine. Fact is, Dante's Inferno describes nothing so terrific. By this time it was raining but the great crowd stuck to the positions as if intent upon devouring us with their eyes. Pretty soon the coaster pulled out down the Deleware river. The April air was chill and damp and having had no sleep for the past two or three days and nights, except such as we could get standing up like a horse, the boys were all soon tucked away in some nice corner and "nature's sweet restorer" in command. After prowling around for some time, we found our way into an elegantly furnished cabin down in the hull of the vessel. It was nicely lighted, with no one in it except Gen. Churchhill and his staff. We selected a kind of out of the way corner, piled some chairs around and spread ourself on the soft carpet to take a nap. We were not long into getting off into dreams of our "home and fair native bowers and pleasures that waited on life's early morn, while memory each scene gaily covered with flowers, revealed every rose but secreted the thorns." Some time after nightfall our boat landed at Ft. Delaware on a little island near the outlet of Delaware bay, some fifty miles from Philadelphia and six or eight miles from the main land. The outfit was marched off the boat without much ceremony. The writer knew nothing of what was going on because of his going ahead with his dreaming. About the time they were all off, two big, burly Yankee home guards found the writer and instead of waking him up like he was a human being, one of them applied his foot, which had on a No. 13 government shoe, to that part of his anatomy where the bosom of his pants wear out first, lifting him up to a standing position, while the other used his bayonet in a very familiar and unlady like manner. We were rattled—they kicked us all the way up the stairway and out to the end of the gang plank. In the confusion incident to such rough handling, we lost our hat, kept our temper and struck the shore with a full head of those feelings peculiar to one loaded down to the guards with equal portions of shy and wild. After all answering to their names we were marched inside the walls. In the absence of better information, we estimate the island on which the fort and barracks were erected, at about fifty acres. The grade was about six feet below high tide and was protected by a levee. The buildings were common board houses, constructed in a square, making a very pretty plaza in the center. Here we were in the hands of officers and men of the regular army, and they treated us with the politeness common between the army officers of nations. At first we were allowed the liberties of the island during the day, that is, the privilege of promenading on the levee. This was not only very clever and refreshing but it afforded us an opportunity to gather shells with which to put sets in rings, breastpins, etc., that we made of gutta percha; but this liberty was soon cut off, because some of the boys buoyed themselves up with canteens, and swam out to the main land and made good their escape back to Dixie, while others would play on the money-loving side of the Yankee and would buy or hire yawls and get away, while some of the Federals would contract to deliver so many safe and sound over on the Delaware side, for so much per head. This, as before hinted, didn't last long and we were confined inside of high walls. The port was commanded by a general by the name of Scheoff. He was a cruel old cuss. Whenever a Confederate made an effort to escape and failed he was then put into a dungeon. The fare at Ft. Delaware was a wretched failure. It consisted of bread, bacon and coffee for breakfast; bacon and bread for dinner and pick-your-teeth for supper. The bread was regular gun-wadding, the coffee was about one grain to every forty gallons of water, and, as to the bacon, it is safe to say it was a lot of sow-belly General Jackson left over after the war of 1812. It was green all the way through and was rank, ranky, rankishly rancid. Our cook was a Confederate who had fallen from grace and had taken up with bad company. We called him Stonewall Jackson and in our mind's eye we can see him now as he tosses in the great big, dirty middlings of bacon into the boiling pot. The meat was then cut into slices about the size of your index finger, laid on a slice of bread the same size and then another was laid on top. These rations were then strung out on a long pine board table, and the door of the dining room was thrown open and we sailed in. Such a thing as beef or any kind of vegetables were not in it. This was the hardest thing we had struck, and that, too, in a country where there was plenty, and the only excuse the United States government can give for thus systematically starving us to death, is that of pure unadulterated cussedness. But for the kindness of Mrs. Cheesborough and other good women of Philadelphia, God only knows how much we would have suffered. As it was, our powers of endurance seemed taxed to their utmost limits; but such is cruel war. During the time we were thus straitened for something to eat, the writer dickered with a Federal soldier for a dozen fresh eggs, and to make sure of getting all the good there was in them, tied a string around the end of one leg of a pair of old pantaloons and held on to the other end while the eggs boiled very hard in the kittle of bacon. We took them out and ate them at one sitting, and the only inconvenience felt was a sort of don't care, dull sort of headache for an hour or two afterwards. There was no ball playing, and very little singing while here. Somehow two or three violins found their way inside the prison; several of the boys could play, and we tripped the light fantastic toe some, but it was stale compared to what it would have been had we had a rebel dressed in calico by our side. We don't remember seeing a woman while on the island. One instance of lack of nerve at the right time, and we are through for this sitting: Lieut. ——— made a dicker with a Federal soldier for a yawl to be delivered at a certain point on the island, paying so much down. The Federal took his money and then went and reported to Gen. Scheoff. About 10 o'clock at night we were all put into line and an officer and the betrayer came down the line looking for the lieutenant. The officer would hold the lantern to each rebel's face as he passed down the line, so that the soldier could identify his man. Just before they got to Lieut. ———, he thought to escape by dropping out and passing in the rear down to that part of the line already inspected. They caught him in the move and he weakened and was sent to the dungeon. His having shaved and changed clothing would have saved him, if he had only had the nerve to have stood shoulder to shoulder with us in line. From this we learn the lesson, that during our natural lives, we lose quite as much by being too smart as we do in not being smart enough, sometimes.

## CHAPTER XII.

ON OUR WAY TO DIXIE — TRIP ON OLD OCEAN'S HOWLING WASTE — FROM FORT DELAWARE TO FORTRESS MONROE — SEA SICKNESS — EXCHANGED AT CITY POINT, VIRGINIA.

On the 29th of April, 1863, we were ordered to get our bag and baggage ready for a trip to Dixie, and never did a piece of good news put more elasticity into the "souls of the sons of men" and more sunshine in their hearts.

By noon we were all in line and marched on board an old coaster, called "The State of Maine." It was not crazy, but from the wear and tear it appeared to have been subject to and the pattern of its build; a guess that it was one of the vessels that escaped the cyclone that cleaned up the Spanish Armada in the year 1521, would not have been extravagant. When time was called for dinner, the plan adopted to feed us was convenient and successful, but the menu was not at all inviting. Our cook,

Stonewall Jackson, had boiled lots of old bacon and cut it up into chunks of about the size of a five cent bar of soap, and shoveled into a hogshead that set on the deck. A hogshead of crackers stood to the left of it, leaving room for us to pass between one at a time. We were formed in line single file, like Indians on the war path, and as we passed between the two, with our right hand we were to grab a chunk of the bacon and with our left all the crackers we could get away with. As a rule, crackers and bacon is good fare for a soldier, and true enough if the quality is all right, but in this instance the crackers were old and chaffy and the bacon rancid all the way through. Some of the boys would run their arms down into it up to their arm-pits in search of a piece that they could eat.

Some time after dinner great volumes of smoke began to boom out from the great chimneys of the vessel, and the steam commenced snapping and hissing, the sailors pulled in the gang plank, the captain tapped the bell and the old steamer pulled out down the bay towards Dixie land, and in bidding good-bye to old Ft. Delaware we wished for one thing only, and that was for about one hundred tons of powder placed about forty feet under the ground near the center of the island, and that we at a safe distance could ignite it and blow the whole outfit into the Atlantic ocean. Nearly a third of a century, however, having swept by since that time, our feelings have gone through quite a mellowing process, and we turn those who so cruelly mistreated us over to the tender mercies of the God of Battles.

About sundown our boat cast anchor at the mouth of the Delaware bay and pretty soon we had all turned in to sleep and dream of table after table loaded with every thing nice to eat and drink we had ever seen or heard of. The reader may think it strange that we write so much of eating and drinking. The logic of this is accounted for in this proposition: Give a soldier plenty to eat, plenty to drink and lots of fighting and " fun " and he is happy. A soldier is a machine; he expects his government to take care of his person, commits his soul to the care of the Great I Am that I Am, and don't worry about that side of his destiny any more.

Early on the morning of the 28th we pulled out on to the booming bosom of the Atlantic.

A description of how sick it made the boys to ride the mad winds and wild waves of old Neptune's duck pond would be a work of supererogation, because the subject was all used up as far back in the dim history of the past as when it made Jonah, the Jew, so sick that he threw up a whale. We stood around on deck in groups learnedly discussing the difference in the shines the boat was cutting and those of a mustang pony when it goes up in the air and returns to earth with its head between its forelegs. We all agreed that the light, gauzy feeling produced in the neighborhood of one's craw were about the same in kind, and the vote was unanimous that we could ride her as long as she kept on her main and tail. We had not gone many knots out of sight of terra firma until the man with his eye on the capers liable to be cut by cause and effect, could very plainly see that old Nep was getting in his work under the lining of lots of the boys' Confederate jackets, and pretty soon you could see them pulling out by ones, twos and threes for their quarters. They were not in the captain's way any more, but lay around loose down in the hold throwing up bacon and crackers and wallowing in it, too sick to live and too much in debt to their stomachs to die. The writer perambulated back toward the stern, lapped his left arm around a post and with his right tossed bits of crackers to big white pigeon-looking birds following the vessel, thinking that this amusement and the cool wind might turn his attention from the sea sickness epidemic that was raging from stem to stern, and from larboard to starboard. While here a long, Florida looking fellow hung the front door of his Confederate commissary store over the banisters just to the right and above us, and the "yaller" bacon greese, lumps of crackers and rebellious bile run out, just as easy. This was just a little too much. Our stomach turned over and tossed up a lot of bacon that burned our throat like straight Georgia whisky going down. We held court right then and there, and discussed the matter of jumping overboard and putting an end to the many ills incident to this sneering, jeering and unfriendly world, but reason or caution suggested that we had better put up with these ills, rather than rush to those in a country we know not of. As soon as hostilities let up a little, we turned loose the post and "lit out" for our bunk way down in the hull of the vessel. We made the landing some time during the evening, a perfect wreck of our former self. From this time on we all done our sitting up laying down. We were too sick to make any note of time, anyway our recollections are that we run in under the big guns at Fortress Monroe late in the evening of April 30, anchored and several Federal officers went on shore. When they returned we asked the news. They had nothing to tell. From their caucussing around in groups and serious talk, we surmised that Lee was giving "fighting Joe Hooker" some trouble. And sure enough he was making "fighting Joe" hunt for the thick brush in the wilderness. This and some other hitch in the cartel for the exchange of prisoners caused us to be held at Fortress Monroe several hours. After much dickering our steamer pulled out into Hampton roads, the battle grounds made historic by the terrific naval engagement between the Merrimac and Monitor. We were soon in the waters of the James river and could see the vine-clad hills of old Virginia. Some time in the afternoon we sighted City Point, and a sure enough Confederate flag as it fluttered in the free, Confederate air from the cedar-clad bluff on the river and all faces were turned towards it. It was the "observed of all observers" and a yell went up from rebel throats such as the impetuous Southerner only can give. For the time our cup of joy was full and the prospects of soon being free again caused strong, brave men to shed tears of gladness. We were, however, let down again, for the big boat cast anchor out in the middle of the river. Then all kinds of rumors commenced to float as to the cause of our being held. Some seemed to take a sort of fiendish delight in getting up big lies and circulating them, and it finally reached the point that we were to be returned to prison because of a failure of the commissioners of exchange to agree on some point. We called a council of war at once and all hands agreed that should the boat head down stream with steam up we would overpower and hog-tie the guards, put them in the hold, run the boat to land and get off, and should the guards resist, we were to fight them to the knife and the knife to the hilt, in a word, we were not going back to prison. Some time during the next day our commissioner, Col. Ould, came down from Richmond in his little boat, and whispered to

Capt. Bob Hopkins and some of the other boys that Lee had cleaned up Hooker. He did this, however, under the pledge that we would make no demonstrations, which pledge we religiously kept. But the yell that was in our throat was so big that it nearly choked us to hold it down. About sundown all the military red tape having been gone through with, we were landed on Dixie soil, boarded a train and in a few hours were turned loose in Petersburg, Virginia.

## CHAPTER XIII.

A FEW DAYS IN RICHMOND — NEW ISSUE OF CONFEDERATE MONEY — OUR NEW SUIT OF MILITARY CLOTHING — WE ARE SHIPPED OUT TOWARD THE SETTING SUN.

We are now out of prison and we had calculated to dismiss our unwritten history of the great war right here, and would have done so, but for the many expressions of appreciation of it, making us bold enough to let our faber have more play. We desire it distinctly understood, that in giving a pen picture of the experiences of the men and officers of the line in the great Army of Tennessee, we do not propose to enter into the discussion of the movements of armies, corps, divisions, brigades, etc., except as they come in incidentally, because an undertaking of this kind would be cutting off larger slices than we have time, ability and disposition to undertake to chew, and, besides, this field has been thoroughly cultivated by President Davis, Gen. J. E. Johnston and other great writers.

In the last chapter we bid our readers good-by at Petersburg, Va., and here the exception to the rule, was to find any of the outfit who had any money, therefore, being turned loose to shift for ourselves in a big city was very little better than being in prison so far as solid comfort was concerned. Some of the boys put on a bold front and put up at the big Bowlingbrook Hotel, while others hung out on the sidewalks and at the city market place. Next morning the outlook improved. We met with no difficulty in the matter of borrowing new issue Confederate money, and the streets being full of old aunty negro hucksters, for one Confederate dollar we could buy a corn dodger and a broiled fish as big and as long as a Chicago girl's foot and two hard-boiled eggs thrown in for good count. After one day we were shipped up to Richmond, and when we arrived we went around to the treasury department and drew twelve months' pay. The writer received $1,080 in new, crisp ten dollar Confederate bills. He felt richer than ever before or since. It was an enormous pile of money — more indeed than we had pocket room for. Richmond at that time, May 2d, 1863, was pretty lively, good hotels, fine restaurants, full stores and jim dandy saloons. The first thing the writer did was to put himself inside of a nice uniform, and after getting it on and standing before a large mirror, admiring the gold bar on our collar, the big brass buttons set in pairs, the curleymacew gold lace on our sleeves, the hat on our head with waving plume, our fine Wellington boots, the new sword that dangled at our side, we had no idea of being able to go two blocks up Main street before we would be offered a position on Gen. Lee's staff or called in as military adviser to President Davis. The reader will have to imagine our utter astonishment at the people in the capitol grounds on Main street, and at the Spotswood paying no more attention to us than to other common mortals. It let us down right smartly, but did not by a large majority seriously impair our opinion of our good looks in our three hundred dollar new suit. While here our headquarters were at Camp Lee, about a mile out from the city. It was here we met our commands, they having been exchanged several days before, and the meeting of officers and men, a recital of experiences since we were separated at St. Louis was touching indeed. As already hinted, our headquarters were at Camp Lee, but having the liberty of the city, and the many good things laying around loose in the great city, out of which a soldier could get lots of solid comfort, kept all the boys on the pad, hardly enough remaining to keep camps. To our minds, all that the women of Richmond lacked of being angels of the first water were the wings, and some of the boys insisted that they had found some whose wings were sprouting. But speaking seriously, the ladies of Richmond treated us with every kindness and marked attention possible. They all wanted a keepsake and we were not long in giving away all the rings we had made while in prison. We were well fixed in Richmond, going at night to see Ogden and the Misses Partington in Macbeth, or to a nice hop at some private residence, hence we were knocked out when the secretary of war ordered our command to report for duty to the commander of the Trans-Mississippi department.

On about May 10, we marched across the high bridge on the James and boarded the cars for a trip towards the setting sun. At Bristol, Tenn., our command was stopped and put into camps. Camp rumor had it that because of some difficulty between Col. Wilks, of the 24th Texas, and Col. Gillespie, of the 25th, concerning which was the ranking officer in the regular line, that the first had reported us in a state of mutiny or insubordination, and that we were to be sent to Gen. Bragg's army to be disciplined. Anyway, we remained here several days. The writer secured a kind of underground leave of absence for the purpose of a few days visit to his old home near Cleveland, Tennessee. We had left there when only twelve years old, and it seemed hard for kinfolks and acquaintances to realize on return a great big young man in a Confederate uniform. A very handsome majority of the people of East Tennessee were what they called "Union Democrats," and while those with whom we were immediately associated, treated us very considerately, we could see that our uniform was distasteful to them. We visited many places where we use to ramble when a little boy; the place where we learned to swim in the little creek. We spent some five or six days in this manner very pleasantly, only one thing happening that caused any bitterness of feeling, and doubtless a lack of proper appreciation of the surroundings by the writer was the cause of that.

## CHAPTER XIV.

AT THE HOME OF OUR BOYHOOD IN EAST TENNESSEE — SOME UNION YOUNG LADIES KNOCK A COUPLE OF TONS OF CONCEIT OUT OF US WITH A BOUQUET.

The little mite of bitterness injected into our sojourn at the old home in East Tennessee, as referred to in the close of the last chapter, came up in this wise: Several solid old farmer Union Democrats treated us right royally in the way of nice dinners, suppers and receptions, and had our experience been as ripe as it is now, and our judgment of men and things as well matured as now, we could have appreciated the fact that they wanted to entertain us as one of their boys and hear us talk as a Texan and not as a soldier. But having just returned from prison, we were neckful of bitterness and war, and as vicious as a rattlesnake in August.

An appointment was made for us to break

bread and eat salt at a Sunday dinner with Mr. Fountain Larrison. Quite a crowd had collected and in the crowd were two or three Miss Clingans visiting the Misses Larrisons. After serving a good dinner, we were all sitting on the long front portico, and the writer was entertaining them, as he thought, by sailing into Grant, Lincoln, Sherman, Union men and the United States government generally, when all at once the young ladies took French leave. We heard them in the parlor tittering and laughing immoderately, but had no idea that they were putting up a job on an officer in his majesty, Jefferson Davis' army, but all doubts on that score were removed when a bouquet about the size of a half-bushel, lit in our lap. In quantity and construction it was all right, but it was made of dog fennel, tanzy, bull nettle, sprigs of oak brush, withered roses and jimson blossoms. It was a pretty deep, keen cut at the time, but as the years roll by and we get on a higher plane from which we survey these things, we see them in a different light. In a word, we were their guest and should have had good manners enough to have had some respect for their opinions. But "what fools these mortals be." This experience should have taught us a lesson, but it seems knocking down was not enough for us. We had to be knocked down and dragged out for we went over to Cleveland the next day and were invited to dinner at the old "Stewart Tavern." It was kept by a preacher by the name of Trim, who had about six old maid daughters, and they were all Andy Johnson Union Democrats, and of course our going amongst them was like putting fire in dry stubble. They had us cornered, and we were fighting right and left, like a loafer wolf, when a long, lean Florida provost-guard stepped in and called for our papers. We had them, but they were out of date. He marched us off to headquarters, and the six girls, when we saw them last, were spread out on the parlor floor laughing as if their hearts would break. We have devoted this much time and space to our personal experience and plead in extenuation of the offense, the disposition we have to tell the truth, that by our experience young men may learn a lesson in common-sense manners. One more instance, however, of how the tail feathers can be pulled from a young man's pride, and we pass along. On our way to Tulahoma, Tenn., to where our command had been ordered, the train stopped at a station called Stephenson, Ala., the conductor, Mr. Russell, came after the writer in hot haste, remarking that a lady wanted to see him. We went with him into the depot. There was a big crowd, it made room for us, and a very pretty woman dressed in black approached with a very pretty bouquet. She made a pretty little speech, eulogizing the Texas troops generally, and those of the Arkansas Post in particular. We stood uncovered of course and received the bunch of flowers, and our vanity said we could make a speech in reply and being in the habit of believing everything. We sailed in; in a loud voice we said: "Fair donor. Ladies and gentle—" this was all there was in us, for we broke down and commenced to bow ourself out of it. We bowed, backed and bowed, and backed until we backed and fell off of the platform and the crowd yelled. While the bouquet was very pretty and smelled sweet yet when we got it into the car we felt like putting it on the floor and jumping on it with all four of our feet. But vanity always goes before a fall.

At Tulahoma, because of the depletions by death and other causes, our command was consolidated. The 6th, 10th, and 15th Texas regiments were made into one and Col. R. Q. Mills was put in command of it. The 17th, 18th, 24th and 25th Texas regiments were made into one and Col. Gillespie was put in command. In the consolidation a great many officers were superannuated and ordered to report to the commander of the Trans-Mississippi department. The writer and W. C. Burris, of McKinney, Texas, were retained; the former was transferred from his company "B" and assigned to duty in company "I," from Johnson County, Texas, while the latter remained with the company. We remained some ten days at Tulahoma in a sort of lay-around-do-nothing state. We were then marched to Wartrace and put into Maj.-Gen. P. R. Cleburne's division; camp rumor had it that no division commander wanted us. Gen. Cleburne interviewed Brig.-Gen. Deshler, our commander, and afterwards had us on review in a meadow near Wartrace, and after running his Irish military eye down our line, said: "This is a fine, handsome looking body of young men, and material out of which good soldiers can be made." At this time our brigade was known as Deshler's Texas Brigade, had just 1,700 men, and we were all between the ages of 21 and 35, all the overs and unders having been let out by reason of the conscript law. And while our brigade was as fine a body of young men as ever was commanded by Napoleon or Wellington, yet no commander wanted us, because as camp rumor had it the surrender at Arkansas Post was a disgraceful affair. They not knowing that three thousand of us had fought forty thousand for two days, to say nothing of a fine fleet of gun-boats.

Brig.-Gen. Woods' Mississippi Brigade of Cleburne's division seemed to take a sort of delight in poking fun at us. They laughed before they were out of the woods; we got it back on them at the battle of Chickamauga, which will come up in this history later on. While at Wartrace, Gen. Cleburne personally supervised the drilling of our brigade. One more instance of how soldiers will get along in camps and try to put on airs and we pass along. Jim Hardin, of Wise County, had foraged around and caught up with a piece of bacon and he and the writer made it up at once to give a dinner to a very few special friends. We viewed an Irish potato patch near by and gathered potato tops with an occasional leaf of lamb's quarter to make up a dish of bacon and greens for dinner, while Jim raided an apple orchard near by for fruit for a pot pie. The apples were about the size of a grape shot, with the bloom still sticking to the end of them. Cold water, flour and the apples as a starter toward our pot pie; boiled the bacon and Irish potato tops and sat down to a regular feast. The dinner was a great success; to some it was like the pills made from the bark of the black walnut when skinned up, to others the bark was skinned down.

## CHAPTER XV.

BRAGG RETREATS FROM SHELBYVILLE AND WARTRACE — FORMS A LINE AT TULAHOMA — SHOWS FIGHT AT ELK RIVER, BUT CROSSES THE CUMBERLAND MOUNTAINS — EXPERIENCE WITH BUSHWHACKERS.

During the month of June, 1863, we were kept on the move, that is, we ate no idle bread. It was one round of duty day in and day out, company drill, regimental and brigade drill, guard mount and inspection, and company roll called five times each day. We Texas fellows "kicked like bay steers" at this; it was hard for the wild western boys to submit to the red tape regularity, and seeming aristocracy of the regular army, for Bragg's army came as near filling the measure of regular troops at this time as any volunteer army ever did. Our brigade commander, A. Deshler, had resigned a captain commission in the U. S. army, his adjutant-general, Joseph T. Hearn, of Galveston, Texas, had a finished military education and was the brigade ideal of an all-round soldier. Lieut. George Jewell filled the place of brigade ordnance officer and he always had the appearance of having just hopped out of a band-box. Our camp was on a nice undulating piece of ground and if the poet, Bryant, puts it right when he says "The groves were God's first temples," the thick, rich foliage of the sugar tree, the beach and the grand oaks that shaded our camp at Wartrace, Tennessee, were his chief of temples. The grounds were kept by order as clean as a new pin, and we almost feel the cool wind to-day as it comes over the meadow down beyond the railroad bridge making wave chase wave in the little field of wheat on the hill-side and putting a flutter in the folds of our flag that has been hanging lazily on its staff at Col. Mills' headquarters. But all this drilling, inspection, dress parade and cleaning of old rusty guns came to an end, for after ten minutes' notice on the morning of June 28th, we had packed our traps and were in line moving with the head of our column going toward Blue Bird Gap. The Federal army under command of Gen. Rosencrans was on the move pressing, we supposed, all along Bragg's front, whose right was somewhere near McMinville and his left at Shelbyville. When our brigade arrived at the Gap already named, quite a lively skirmish was going on. We were put in line in a wheat field on the safe side of a hill. Woods' Mississippi Brigade were in line a few spaces lower down the hill and in our rear. The Texas boys here got in some work on the "mud-heads" as we called them. The ground was covered with a sort of iron ore pebbles; the Texans would flip these pebbles right over the heads of the Mississippians in such manner as to make them sing like a minnie ball, and they stuck their heads so close to the ground that their mustaches took root and commenced to grow. We had fun enough for all until they caught us in the trick. That night we were marched back to the camp we had left in the morning; passing through a little town called Bellbuckle, on the 29th the whole army seemed to be on the move towards Tulahoma. On July 1st, Bragg strung out his long line of infantry in front of Tulahoma as if he intended to make fight, but after waiting and watching all day, no enemy appearing, late in the evening we were put on the move again and to our astonishment in the direction of Chattanooga. About day light we crossed Elk river and went into camps footsore, weary and out of humor generally, then commenced the figuring by all the boys as to what was the matter that the great army of Tennessee should be retreating. The conclusion was pretty generally reached that old Rosencrans was flanking us, but this did not satisfy, for the boys insisted that if he flanked us why in the Hades couldn't we flank him, and by the way it seems to us yet that there was some good philosophy in the idea especially in the light of the way the thing panned out. About 3 o'clock in the evening we were ordered to recross the river, and move back toward the enemy. This suited us, for we were red hot for a fight. We traveled about two miles and formed a line of battle at right angles to and across the big road. The enemy were advancing cautiously in line and everything indicated that the ball would open right there. Col. Mills made us a speech. We remember one sentence of it, it ran something like this: " Texas cavalry on the right, Texas cavalry on the left, a Texas battery in the center, all supported by Texas Infantry and who dare come against us."

A little brush on our left by the cavalry about sundown was all there was in it. About an hour after dark we moved out, and as we crossed the long wooden bridge on the river we noticed several piles of rich pine split very fine and laid on it. We knew that this spelled that it would be burned as soon as we got through with it in order to delay the Yankees in their forward movement. We marched all night and about 12 o'clock on July the 4th we stopped to rest at the foot of the rock ribbed and ancient Cumberland mountain. Here the writer had a chill and consequently high fever. Getting permission to march at will from Dr. Stuart, our regimental surgeon, we lost sight of the boys for several days, for notwithstanding we were sick enough to be "abed," we out-traveled them by a fine majority, and besides they were delayed in guarding our supply train. We remember passing a place on the mountain called Polk's University Place. The trip was a rough experience for a sick man, but we had it down that we were not going to be captured, and we counted every step as one more in the direction or getting out of the way. About noon on the fifth we marched down a deep gorge, by a big blue spring that was boiling with cold water enough to float an ordinary steamboat; a little further on we came to a comfortable looking farmhouse. We were so sick and worn out that we went into the yard and laid down on the grass in a deep shade with our mind made up to stop there until we got well, died or was captured by the Yankees. From where we were lying we could see a little field up near the spring, and the wheat was yet in the shocks; several teamsters went in with a view of getting forage for their teams. The Union or some other kind of bushwhackers fired on them from above in the thick woods on the side of the mountain. This put a new spur in our head and two on our heels, cooled our fever and gave us a new pair of legs, for if there is anything that a regular soldier has a holy, healthy horror for it is a bushwhacker. We climbed over the fence and was just moving off when one of the 11th Texas cavalry came along on foot; he broke open the farmer's stable and borrowed two pretty good horses. We asked him if a divide wouldn't be the correct thing, he said he thought not, "for horseback riding was liable to make an infantryman's head swim, however, I might ride one of them as long as we traveled the same road."

## CHAPTER XVI.

CROSSING THE TENNESSEE RIVER — GEN. HARDEE JUMPS IN THE RIVER AFTER A WILD TEXAN — WE FIND A MOONSHINER — THE COMMENCEMENT OF THE CHICKAMAUGA CAMPAIGN.

We are yet away from our command, and to continue our reminiscence will necessarily have to deal in personal experiences until we strike it again. Pretty early the next morning we came to the Tennessee river; our haversack was in a distressingly lean condition, and we were yet sick, the flux having joined in with the fever and chills, and strange as it may seem, yet it is no stranger than true, that a big bait of half ripe apples cured us sound and well. We sloshed around in the orchard all day, slept in an old out-house at night, and went on our way the next morning well, hearty and as gay as any soldier in the Confederacy. Pretty soon we came to where pontoons were laid across the great Crooked river, and just as we expected the provost-guard were taking up all who proposed crossing, and herding them until their command came up. They were having some difficulty in holding them. We all wanted to get the river between us and the Yankees, just as quick as possible. This we account for on the hypothesis, the longer and further a soldier retreats, the more earnest he gets in the matter, and the harder it is for him to find a place where he thinks it is safe to make a stand. Our corps commander, Gen. Hardee, was there; a long, keen Texas soldier said he was going over anyhow; when he started, Gen. Hardee drew his sword and made a dive at him. The fellow jumped into the river and the General plunged in after him on horseback. This created some excitement and no little amusement for the boys, and while all eyes were turned to the general and the private, we walked on to the bridge and crossed over, went up to the hill and down the big road whistling a tune of childish joy. Pretty soon our educated forage eyes discovered a trail leading off down through the great woodland. We walked therein and "got there Eli," with both feet; after going about a mile we came to a big blue Tennessee spring, and while standing and watching the cool blue water boil up we heard a noise just above us in the thick brush on the hill-side. Says I, "what are you doing up thar?" "It's none of yer business," says he. "Well, we will see about that thar," says I. We climbed around the bluff up to where he was, and to our astonishment and exceedingly great joy we found him to be an East Tennessee moonshiner. The scales dropped from over our eyes at once, and we could reasonably account for the trail we had been traveling being worn as slick as an otter slide. He had a keg of very fine corn whisky, we sampled it over and again; for a five dollar Confederate bill he filled our quart canteen, and when we slung it around our neck, he bade us good-day with the remark: "Go on your way, and tell no man." We had not gone many leagues before we were seriously discussing the matter of suggesting to President Davis the propriety of relieving Gen. Bragg and putting us in command of the army. We foraged around over the country generally during the day and at nightfall we went into camps with the boys under the shadow of Lookout mountain. After two or three days' rest, we were shipped on the cars and went into camps near Tyners station, on the Chattanooga & Cleveland Railway. Here we were put through the same hard drilling and camp routine of duty as at Wartrace. This was the second time the army of Tennessee had been camped in the country about Chattanooga, hence it was an exceedingly lean country so far as good foraging was concerned, no hogs, no sheep, no goats, no chickens. We could not even " get a piece of bacon for a sick captain." While here Serg. George Dean and Corpl. J. P. Fullingim, of Company " B " were sent with a squad of men to guard an important bridge on the Chickamauga. The weather was warm, Dean and Fullingim spread their blankets for a sleep on the high grade near the end of the bridge, yet out of the way of the train. Away in the night, while they were sound asleep dreaming of conquering the enemy and of being promoted to captains and colonels, and being put in command of such posts as Boston and New York, a train came dashing along; they mistook it for a charge of Federal cavalry and jumped from the high bridge some forty feet into the creek below. It was a miracle that they were not killed, but they were not to go that way. An instance of how men will get scared and stampede like cattle will come up in these reminiscences later on. After about twelve days at Tyners' Station our division was marched to old Harrison, the original county site of Hamilton County, Tennessee, to do picket duty on the river. The change suited us to a "T," for the foraging was better in the valley farms of the river. We found plenty of ripe sweet potatoes, green corn, and garden truck, and while the orders forbidding foraging were strict, and the provost guard on the watch, yet we managed to beat them all and lived fine. While here several of us run the gauntlet and went over into the old, very old city. A Union widow lady and her seven grown daughters kept the hotel for the city. We ordered dinner for our crowd and got it; but it did not stay with us, for these good Union ladies either by mistake or on purpose put something in it that made us all deathly sick for an hour or two. We humped and bucked around there like Spanish ponies, in our efforts to throw it up; medical men may know what it was when we say that it so affected our eyes that there were two of everything we looked at; we all got over it and did not tell it when we returned to camps. The joke was too good to tell.

On the morning of September 5th, 1863, we commenced the first move that culminated in the great battle of Chickamauga, just fourteen days afterwards. Our division was marched back to Tyners' Station, and that night to Chattanooga. The weather was exceedingly warm, and an all day and quite all night forced march was pretty trying on us. The roads were very dusty, and in avoiding it the men would march in the hog trails, and by ways on each side of the big road. The writer was following along after a fellow by the name of Geo. Couch, of the 18th regiment; the dirt road approached the railroad diagonally; as it came in on our right, by the star-light, we mistook the cut in the railroad for another dirt road. Couch walked off into it and fell some twenty feet, breaking his collar-bone, as well as shaking him up generally. A guard was placed there at once, or no telling how many of the boys would have tumbled into a ditch they did not dig. On we went through Chattanooga, and were halted some time between midnight and daylight at the base of Lookout Mountain, on the morning of the 6th, footsore and weary. Our division moved up the valley and rested at night near the Crawford Springs.

The idea of our army giving up the city of Chattanooga, the gate to the center of the Confederacy, was trying on our confidence in Gen. Bragg and all others in authority over us, and the saying of all the boys was: "If we can't check them and whip them with the advantages of the river and the mountain-locked passes on the right and left of Chattanooga, where is the place we can?" And this added to the recent fall of Vicksburg made the outlook gloomy indeed.

On the 16th, Bragg's army with the exception of Buckner's division, which was marching from Bull's Gap, was massed between Lafayette, Georgia and McLemors' Cove. At this time, we boys had it that three corps of Rosencrans army were distributed along the Tennessee as follows: McCook at Old Harrison, twenty-five miles above Chattanooga; Crittenden at Chattanooga, and Thomas at Bridgeport, twenty-five miles below Chattanooga; but we are invading the province of the sure enough historian and must content ourself with chopping it off with a promise of a description of the miscarriage of Bragg's well laid plans in the McLemors' Cove move in our next chapter.

## CHAPTER XVII.

BRAGG ABANDONS CHATTANOOGA — HIS FAILURE TO BAG THOMAS AT M'LEMORE'S COVE NECESSITATES THE GREAT BATTLE OF CHICKAMAUGA.

Doubtless, Bragg moving out his army in such hot haste, and abandoning such a naturally strong position as the Chattanooga line was an open confession to Gen. Rosencrans of his inability to give him battle, and made him very eager to catch up with us. Now McLemore's Cove is a section of country of some several thousand acres locked in by high mountains with only three passes, two of which we held, the one to the southeast and the other outlet to the northeast. Gen. Thomas with an estimated force of 16,000 Federals crossed the river and marched into the Cove through the south pass, on the morning of the 10th, Gen. Bragg deployed Polk's Corps on the left, and Hardee's on the right, covering the two passes already named, while Gen. Hindman with a division made a detour to the right, with an old citizen as guide, to cover the gap through which Gen. Thomas had come, thus having him entirely cut off. We write thus boldly concerning these great movements of the army, because of speaking advisedly. The writer had the honor of being on pretty intimate terms with Maj. Dickson and Capt. Buck of Gen. Cleburne's staff, and besides all of the boys seemed in some sort of way to fully understand the situation; but to return. Gen. Hindman's guide either misled him intentionally or he was not acquainted with the country, and Hindman's command failed to reach the gap on time, and when Polk and Hardee's troops moved on Thomas at the appointed time, he "picked himself up and moved out pell-mell through the gap he had come in at. This trifling mistake by Hindman saved sixteen thousand Yankees from being captured and made the great battle of Chickamauga necessary, besides causing the loss of Chattanooga." The Yankees left in such hot haste they left lots of good picking for us. After nightfall, footsore, weary and disappointed, we marched back to the highlands where we had left on the morning. Our brigade slept on their arms on a small strip of ground between the big road and a high rail fence, and right here occurred an instance of how men will stampede like cattle. We were all in a sound sleep; just across the road some horses and mules were tied to caissons and portable forges; they got to kicking and fighting and rattled their chains. The boys all seemed to wake at the same time, and each fellow thought that the camps were full of loose horses running over and trampling people to death, and each fellow seemed to think that his neighbor was a loose horse, and we pitched into fighting each other with our blankets, sticks or anything we could get our hands on. Everybody was hallooing "whoa," "whoa." The writer tried to climb a black oak tree near by that was at least four feet over and fifty feet to the first limb. Captain J. A. Formwalt, our company commander, had backed himself up against it and he said he knocked us down three times before he could keep us from climbing right over him. In the wild rush we tore down the high fence, run over Lieut. Bartow and broke his right arm, besides crippling several others. Just inside the fence was an orchard, and after quiet had been restored, we found several of the boys perched like fighting chickens up in the apple trees, and yet sound asleep; this is a pretty strong one, rather too heavy to go down slick and easy, therefore we refer to such eye-witnesses as Lieut. W. B. Brown, Hugh McKenzie, C. A. Williams, C. L. Smith, all of Denton, Texas, T. J. Cartwright and J. P. Fullingim, of Wise County, and Col. R. Q. Mills, of Corsicana. After two days we were moved back in the direction of Chattanooga, and took a position at Bluebird Gap, in the Mission ridge range. It was here we got a good look at Gen. Jno. C. Breckenridge of Kentucky. He was the finest looking man we saw during the war. Friday morning, the 18th of September, everything seemed to be moving back towards Chattanooga. We were moving north, there was quite a high wind blowing, the dust in the road was deep, making it very disagreeable; in the evening we could hear heavy cannonading away to the right. We slept on our arms. Saturday the 19th, about 12 o'clock, our line was put in motion, moving slowly northward down on the east of Chickamauga; the cannonading was kept up all day, growing more terrific in the evening, the boys all looked serious, few were the jokes cracked, all realized that blood was going to be shed and the ground torn up in that neighborhood pretty soon. About five o'clock we could hear the musketry. Now we are wading the swift cold Chickamauga, now in a double quick, and just as the blood-red sun seemed to rest on top of Mission Ridge, taking a last look for the day at the two great armies of one blood and one nation, as they were in battle array against each other, we were swung into line of battle on Cheatham's left, and just as soon as our line dressed to the right we moved forward. It was now quite dark, but we struck the Federal line and moved it. The right of our brigade got mixed up with them in the darkness and captured many prisoners. This ended the battle for the day. We lay in line of battle all night; the ground we occupied had been fought over several times during the day; the dead and wounded were all about us all night we could hear the wounded between ours and the Federal lines calling some of their comrades by name and begging for water. The night was cold and crisp, and the dense woodland was dark and gloomy; the bright stars above us and flickering light from some old dead pine trees that were burning in an old field on our left and in front, giving every thing a wierd, ghostly appearance. The writer found a dead Federal soldier near our company line; we felt around in the darkness and found his gun; we relieved him of his cartridge box and sixty rounds of ammunition, and fitting it to our own waist, we felt prepared for the work on the morrow. Those of our readers who have had the strength of their nerves tried by going into battle armed with a little wrought iron sword only, can appreciate how we felt when armed with a good gun and plenty of ammunition. The Federal line was about four hundred yards from ours, and all night long we could hear them felling the big poplar and pine trees, from behind which they would fight us the next day. Our line was changed several times during the night, and notwithstanding we had slept but little, and had been on the march for the last fourteen days and nights, sleep seemed to have gone from our eyes, and slumber from our eyelids, and as we lay there with our faces turned up towards the heavens watching the bright stars and listening to the twitter of the little birds in their nests in the wildwood, many, many, many a soldier asked himself the question, what is all this about? Why is it that one hundred and twenty thousand men of one blood and one tongue, believing as one man in the fatherhood of God and the universal brotherhood of man should in the blaze of the civilization of the nineteenth century of the Christian era, be thus armed with all the improved appliances of modern warfare and seeking each other's lives? The truth of the matter is just this, many a soldier on both sides said to himself and his next friend, if you will pick out the man or men that I have to whip or kill if this thing goes on, we can settle the matters of differences by compromising, and all be at home in ten days. During the night Longstreet's corps of Lee's army arrived and took up position on our left. The disposition of Bragg's army at this time, as well as we boys could locate it, was Gen. Leonidas Polk's corps of Louisiana, Tennessee and Georgia troops on the right, Gen. D. H. Hill's corps of Texas, Arkansas and Mississippi troops in the center, and Gen. Longstreet's on the left.

## CHAPTER XVIII.

#### THE GREAT BATTLE OF CHICKAMAUGA.

Sunday morning, September the 20th, 1863, the sun came up bright and cheery from over on the other side of the Blue Ridge, and the reflection on the autumn leaves as their shadows danced in the clear waters of the Chickamauga, tinged the great woodland in amber and gold. The boys all looked serious and determined, doubtless appreciating the fact, that before the sun went out of sight on the other side of Missionary Ridge and Lookout Mountain, that many of them will have crossed over the river, and their spirits gone up from amidst the din and smoke of battle, to the home of good soldiers and patriots beyond the stars.

After a breakfast, on blue Florida beef, corn bread washed down with cold water, and our canteens filled with Adam's ale, we were in line impatiently waiting for the worst that might come, for a certainty of something bad falling to our lot is preferable to suspense after reaching a certain point incident to long watching and waiting. The writer yet had his gun, and discovered that several captains and lieutenants had fitted themselves with gun and ammunition. Pretty soon one who seemed to have the right kind of authority came down the line and disarmed us, leaving us nothing to go to battle with but our little straight Confederate sword, so dull that it wouldn't cut cheese and too blunt to stick into a stack of hay. If David's sword had been as dull as ours, he would have been sawing on the tough neck of old Goliah to this good day. Why all this delay? The fact is the battle was to begin at daylight and here it is 9 o'clock and everything away to the right, where Polk was to bring on the attack at daylight, is as quiet as a May morning. But here, something is going to happen now. Here comes the "old war horse" himself, General Bragg riding down and inspecting his lines of battle. The boys feel that the moments are big with events; they tightened their belts, pulled their hats well down on their heads, and at the command, right dress, all elbows touch to the right as if on dress-parade. As the boom of the big cannon off to the right dies away against the rock-ribbed sides of Missionary Ridge, the command, "forward march," came down the line from the right, and as the sound of musketry came from the right our army seemed to be advancing in echelon by brigade. Capt. Rhodes Fisher of Austin, Texas, commanding company "G" of the 6th, 10th and 15th Texas regiments, advanced in front of our regiment as skirmishers. Several from Denton County, Texas, were members of this company. We well remember Sergt. Dick Harper; he had a foghorn voice. We could hear him repeat the commands after Capt. Fisher above all others. Dick was a mere boy but a soldier on every part of the ground. Woods' Mississippi brigade was on our right. As we advanced the boys would salute strange soldiers as we passed them and crack jokes as if feeling relieved at the certainty of ending the campaign, one way or the other pretty soon. We were moving in the line of battle, at least four hundred pieces of artillery were booming, the earth seemed to be trembling under this and the tread of the mighty armies. The enemy's skirmishers are run in. Capt. Fisher's company had rallied on the center and resumed their place in the regiment. On we go. All at once an artillery officer comes down the line on horseback, going at a speed as if shot from a cannon, giving the command as he passed: "By the right flank, double quick, march!" We were going nearly on a run, just now a cannon-ball cuts a pine tree down, striking it some forty feet from the ground; it fell lengthwise on Capt. Rhoades Fisher's company, and strange to say, it did not cripple any one seriously. After moving to the right about the length of our brigade, we were halted, line dressed and moved forward. We were thus moved to the right under fire in this sort of hot haste to fill a gap caused by Wood's Mississippi brigade giving away. This was the outfit that had poked so much fun at us Texas fellows, and the boys seemed to enjoy it as a good joke on the mud-heads. Pretty soon we were brought to a halt, close by where the writer was lying down. Gen. Longstreet was sitting on his horse; we did not know who he was, he having no mark of an officer about him, wearing a common hunting shirt and a slouch hat. Ad Anderson of the Wise County Company "B" had been on the front and used his gun until it got so foul that it choked; he came back leisurely and passed through our line, when Gen. Longstreet said to him: "Hello, my good fellow, you are not going to leave us, are you?" Ad stopped and looked up at him and said, "See here, you d— old hunting-shirt snoozer, do you know who you are talking to?" Longstreet laughed heartily at the reply, explained who he was; he and Private Anderson quit good friends. Anderson was about six feet four inches, and as brave as Gen. Longstreet or anybody else. Pretty soon we were ordered forward, and as we reached the crest of the hill in our front, we struck the same sawyer that had knocked Woods' brigade out at the first round. The rain of lead that the Federals poured into our line was simply terrific. Our loss in officers and men for the first few minutes was alarming in the extreme. Capt. Jack Leonard, late banker at Dallas, Texas, commanding Company "E," lost in killed and wounded twenty-eight men, out of a company of about fifty. This seemed to be a key or the turning point in the great battle, and we were ordered to lie flat down and hold it. In a very short time the men were out of ammunition. The writer was ordered by

Capt. J. A. Farmwalt of Hood County to report the fact to Col. Mills. Mills ordered us to report to Brig.-Gen. Deshler. We went in search of Gen. Deshler and found him on the line to our right, down on his hands and knees, as if trying to see below the smoke and discover the position of the enemy. When we were in about ten feet of him and before we had delivered the order a bomb shell struck and killed him instantly. We reported the fact at once to Col. Mills and he took command of the brigade and directed its movements with marked skill and cool bravery the remainder of the day. We held the position until Polk's corps turned the enemy's left and Longstreet his right. A general rout of the whole Federal army occurred just before sun-down, and we never were as glad of anything before nor since in all our long line of experience; and when the stars came out everything was as quiet as death on the field of Chickamauga. We went into camps on the battle-field while the Yankees were running over each other in their wild efforts to get into Chattanooga and to put the Tennessee river between " we 'uns and you un's."

## CHAPTER XIX.

A DAY ON THE FIELD OF CHICKAMAUGA AFTER THE GREAT BATTLE — WE SEE MANY WONDERFUL THINGS — THE HORRORS OF WAR.

The blood red sun has gone down over beyond the great range of mountains, deep darkness has spread its mantle over the field of Chickamauga, and the heart sinking silence that prevailed after the great battle, is disturbed only by the groans of the wounded and the hum of the many voices as the soldiers would in deep tones inquire for missing comrades, and earnestly congratulate each other upon the success of the day.

Our brigade was moved a little way back towards Chickamauga creek, and went into camps. We were yet on the battle-field; the dead in gray and blue were around us on every hand. It has always been a mystery to us, why Gen. Bragg had his army to remain on the field twenty-four hours after the battle had ended. The sickening sight we saw there, of men wounded, and mangled in every way imaginable, was certainly enough to convince all, that war is a cruel thing, and an unnatural way of settling difficulties, and that the civilization of this age of the world, should take it by the beard and drive it back to its native hell. But the question as to whether there is such a thing as a righteous war, has nothing to do with this writing at this time. Our aim being as before remarked, and hinted at in our head lines, is to give the unwritten history of the experiences of the private soldiers and officers of the line, with whom we were associated for three years, three months and twenty-five days. Strange as it may seem, yet no stranger than true, we spread our home-made blankets and slept sweetly and soundly on the field of death that Sunday night. We remained there all day Monday. Monday morning bright and early the writer borrowed a staff-officer's horse, ostensibly for the purpose of going to Chickamauga creek for several canteens of water, but really to take a ride over the battle-field. We were out some five or six hours on horseback, and put in the remainder of the day traveling over the field on foot, and now reader, " listen, and we will to thee a tale unfold, whose lightest word will harrow up thy soul, freeze thy blood. Make thy two eyes, like stars, start from their spheres. Thy knotted and combined locks to part; and each particular hair to stand on end, like the quills upon the fretful porcupine." As indicated in the last chapter, the Federals had felled many of the big pine and poplar trees in such a manner as to afford them splendid protection; and from behind this sort of protection we had to charge and drive them, and the wonder to this day is, how did we do it? Fact is none but the impetuous hot blooded Southern soldiers could have done it. Our loss was necessarily large, and the results as they panned out afterwards, made it a very high-priced victory. But we must return to the matter of telling what we saw on the battle-field. We saw men cold and stiff in death, and yet holding on to their gun; some with the ramrod yet in their hand; some with paper yet between their teeth, just as they had bitten it from the cartridge for loading, and the cartridge yet held by their thumb, middle and forefinger as if in the act of emptying the powder into their gun. On that part of the field where the Tennessee troops had such a terrific battle with Michigan troops, supporting a steel battery of twelve guns, we found many things to wonder at. A Federal had been wounded in the knee, had crawled behind a log, was sitting with back to it, and was binding up his wound, when he was shot in the head; his head dropped over on his shoulder; he remained sitting with his hands yet holding to the linen he was trying to bind his wound with. Hard by him we found a very fine looking dog riddled with bullets. Just across the road we found a Confederate, still in death, yet sitting with his back against a tree, his eyes blared wide open. We found several dead rabbits and birds. We found one man with his brains between his feet, a cannon ball had struck him so as to lift his entire head off, and as he fell his brains fell between his feet; the lining or covering for them was not broken. We found some of the big logs from behind which the Federals fought, just bristling with ramrods: we account for this on the ground that we rebels were in such hot haste while advancing, shooting and loading, that we did not take time to return the ramrods to their place but let the Federals have ramrods and all. We saw many whose hands and arms were in the exact position of holding their guns taking aim. We saw many who had been stripped of all their clothing, and many whose pockets had been rifled and turned inside out. Men were wounded in every shape and place imaginable. Boone Daugherty, of Denton, and a member of Company G., of the 18th Texas regiment says he is going back there one of these days to see "if the thirteen teeth the Yankees pulled for him and planted there have sprouted and produced any of their kind."

By noon Monday the stench from dead men and horses was getting to be sickening. By sundown on the 21st the wounded had all been cared for and the dead buried. Monday night we moved in the direction of Chattanooga. Bragg seemed to move his army as leisurely as if there was no such thing as time affording the enemy an opportunity to get in good shape to receive him when he arrived at Chattanooga. On the morning of the 23d, Bragg's army crossed over Missionary Ridge and formed a line extending from the Tennessee river above around the city of Chattanooga to the river below, taking possession of Lookout Mountain. Bragg bluffed around for two days as if he would hurl his already wounded and broken army against the strong forts that we had constructed around Chattanooga with our own hands. The mistake of Gen. Bragg's life was in not crowding the Federals while they were whipped and demoralized, and going into Chattanooga with them. Gen. Bragg sending out sounders to find out what the rank and file thought of charging the works around Chattanooga was a clear indication of his weakness, and Old Granny methods of thought. The excuse put up that the Confederates were too much exhausted to follow up the victory at Chickamauga on Sunday night, will not hold water, because the Federals had been marched just as hard as we had, and they not only got to Chattanooga that night, but all the means for crossing the river had to be destroyed to keep them from crossing over and pulling out every man on his own hook toward Nashville. Had Forrest or some young man been in command, the results of the victory at Chickamauga would have been better for the Confederacy. But enough of this "I told you so," business. Bragg, Polk, Hindman, Hill, Hardee, Longstreet, Cheatham, Cleburne and Forrest have answered roll-call in the great camps beyond the river, and are resting under the shade of the trees, and the historian will come up far enough removed from those stirring days to impartially locate the blame.

## CHAPTER XX.

SIX WEEKS IN FRONT OF CHATTANOOGA — HEAVY PICKET DUTY — HELL'S HALF ACRE — BIG GAME OF DRAW POKER — SIGNAL SERVICE.

As already intimated, after two or three days waltzing around in the valley, our line settled down, extending from the river above the city, of Chattanooga, from a point quite northeast of the city around south at the base of Missionary Ridge to a point quite northwest of the city, taking the high point of Lookout mountain commanding the river and railroads above and below the city, and the only route remaining over which the Federal army could get supplies was by wagons on dirt roads over Waldon's Ridge. Being in the immediate presence of the enemy, we beat the Confederacy out of about six weeks' drilling. We put in a part of September, October and a part of November in guard duty. The writer's brigade was near the center of the line. Guard duty was pretty trying; our line of pickets was about two hundred yards from the Federal line; we could see their pickets plainly, and when no big officer on either side was near, we would sometimes get up a temporary armistice, lay down our arms and meet on half way grounds and have a nice friendly chat, swapping our flat tobacco for Lincoln coffee, our little 8x10 newspaper, "The Chattanooga Rebel," for their big blanket-sheet dailies, such as the New York Herald, Tribune, Cincinnati Times and Louisville Journal. Sometimes we would strike Federals on duty who would have none of us; these were generally Pennsylvania troops. We could always get along with Ohio and other western troops, but those first named and all other eastern troops always seemed to have a big red mad on.

Our bill of fare was pretty tough; corn-bread and poor beef was about all we had as a rule, and when the rule was suspended, it was generally by a day's rations of bacon. The writer's mess consisted of Capt. J. A. Farmwalt of Hood County, Texas, and Lieut. Jerry Johnson of Johnston County; Lieut. John Willingham belonged to it but he was generally at regimental headquarters acting as adjutant; we kept a cook hired, by the name of Ad Huffstuttler, at $30.00 per month in Confederate money; guess he was a Dutchman by his name, anyway he could forage and cook like one; he would prowl around the butcher pen, get beef heads, feet, liver, brains, sweet-breads, marrow, gut and other parts that we had always seen thrown away and make up messes nice enough for a king. He also done our washing and mending. When the day for the draw of old Ned came around as the boys called it, Capt. Farmwalt would be our head cook; he would fry the grease out of the bacon, and with our corn-bread, water and the grease, make a dish he called " cush;" this with some of the corn-bread burned to a black crisp, out of which we made coffee, was fine living; however, we " reckon" the hard exercises each day and the total absence of anything like dyspepsia or indigestion was what made it all go down so well.

It doubtless seems to the reader that the same routine of duty each day and night would get to be distressingly monotonous, but not so, there was something to be done every day, or some news going the rounds, and when not on guard duty, nor on the fatigue party list, nor putting some finishing touch in making our quarters more comfortable, and not writing letters home, or to two or three Georgia girls at the same time, we could go down to Hell's half acre. Now this was a place in front of and near the center of our main line, and just in rear of our picket line, it being some three quarters of a mile in front of our line of battle. Here the thugs, thumpers and gamblers from our army as well as from Atlanta and other cities collected to gamble, and you could get a square up and up whack at any kind of game from faro, monte, draw-poker, seven-up, down to thimble ring poker-dice and three card monte. We don't know where the boys got the money, but they had stacks of gold, silver, greenbacks and Confederate. The place should have been called Hell's whole acre, for they had about that much ground worn as slick as glass, and more gambling going on than we have ever seen at one time since; and more hard looking characters,—the Five Points of New York City could not beat it even in its palmiest days. While here President Davis paid us a visit. His presence did not create any perceptible enthusiasm in the army; the thoughtful men could plainly see that the grand army of Tennessee under Gen. Braxton Brágg had lost its grip. During our stay here, the Texas Brigade was reorganized, the 7th Texas infantry, B. H. Granbury, colonel, and K. M. Van Zandt as major was put in it, with Dr. Lawrence, of Statesville, N. C., as regimental surgeon and Dr. C. Lipscomb, of Denton, Texas, assistant surgeon. The 3rd and 5th Confederate regiments of Memphis, Tenn., commanded by Col. Cole, were also put in our brigade. The last named regiments were Irish, and soldiers of the first water. It used to be a treat to us boys to happen around about the time of their roll-call and hear the names, O'Parion, O'Flarity, O'Flemsey and O'Connels called. But when it came to standing in their place in battle, playing cards when in camps and stealing when on the march, they were Jeems as well as Joe Dandies. The Brigade was now made up of the following regiments: 6th, 10th and 15th regiments consolidated, commanded by Col. R. Q. Mills; 7th Texas infantry, commanded by Col. H. G. Granbury; 17th, 18th, 24th and 25th consolidated Texas regiment, commanded by Lieut.-Col. John T.

Coit, of Dallas, Texas; 3rd and 5th Confederates, commanded by Col. Cole, of Memphis, and all commanded by Brig.-Gen. J. A. Smith, of Alabama, with Capt. J. T. Hearn, A. A. G., George Jewell, brigade ordnance officer, and D. F. Stewart, brigade surgeon. And if Bragg had had fifty thousand like us and the ability to command, he could have marched to Cincinnati and remained there.

From where we were on the line we could see the Lookout plainly. Just on the high point next to the river, we had a battery, and opposite it, and across the river on Mocason Point, the Federals had a fort. They fought an artillery duel nearly every day while we were here. The boys with mathematical turn of mind would figure on the distance from where we were to the top of the mountain by the time it required the sound to reach us after we could see the flash of the big guns. Don't remember the distance now, but it was several miles away, and in our mind's eye "Horatio" we can see the mountain to-day as it reared its head away up in the clouds, grand, gloomy, silent, looking down in its awe-inspiring majesty upon us poor puffed up mortals. 'Tis sunset at Chattanooga now, and as we stand uncovered, and drink in the magnificence of the surroundings, our very soul sinks within us, when the thought rolls up in our mind, that the years and centuries will go by, and all these who are actors in this great drama will have gone back to dust, and Lookout mountain will yet remain to greet the eyes of millions coming after us. Now the stars are out, and the line of red lights from the high point of Lookout mountain. Along our line away to the extreme right is the Signal corps reporting every movement of the enemy; in daylight this was done by red and white flags. The scene is grand and is many leagues beyond our powers of description. The October evening is warm, we spread our blankets, lay down with our face turned toward the shining stars and wonder how, when and where all this foolishness will come to an end, and as the last notes from the brass throat of the brigade bugler's horn sounding tattoo dies away in the silence of the night we commit our soul in prayer to the care of the God of battles, and our weary body to the arms of nature's sweet restorer.

## CHAPTER XXI.

### BATTLE OF MISSIONARY RIDGE, TENNESSEE.

In a few days after the battle of Chickamauga, Gen. Longstreet was sent with his corps and some other troops to drive Gen. Burnside outside of Knoxville! Gen. Wheeler with a large cavalry force was sent out on a raid into middle Tennessee, while Gen. Bragg seemed to be content to wait there at Chattanooga long enough for the enemy to get supplies and concentrate a force sufficient to come out, attack and clean up his army.

On the evening of November 23d, our division was put in motion moving in the direction of Cleveland. We marched about eight miles, went into camp and it is said were waiting for transportation by railroad to Knoxville. At this time Gen. Grant was in command of the Federal army, and as soon as Bragg moved out our division (Cleburne's) he commenced at once to press our line. Gen. Grant had a big army in Chattanooga, while Gen. Joe Hooker had a force at Bridgeport, some twenty-five miles or less below Chattanooga. All night of the 23d Gen. Bragg had details of men to keep up fires on that part of the line we had left, beating drums as if he had a big force on that part of the line; but Gen. Grant was too old a bird to be caught with that kind of chaff, and just kept on pressing. While it was yet dark, on the morning of the 24th, our division was moved back and took position just in rear of our old line, and east of the ridge. The writer with permission went to the top of the ridge, and from where we were, we could see over the whole valley, and it was alive and working with long lines of blue infantry, bristling with bayonets; it was a fine view of the pomp and splendor of glorious war, and we felt it in our very bones, that the ground was going to be torn up and lots of people hurt in the neighborhood before many days. All at once, about 4:30 in the afternoon, we were put in line and started off at a double quick, to the right. We knew from the way couriers were dashing around, the serious expression on the face of those in high place, the haste with which we were being moved, and the old decks of playing cards the boys ahead of us were throwing away, that somebody was getting hurt, or we were on a race with the Federals for some important point. Referring to the playing cards, it is strange that men will carry something in their pockets they are ashamed to be found dead with. We had seen this throwing of cards away before. But enough of this. On we go ;. we crossed the mountain right over the Chattanooga and Cleveland Railroad tunnel, and formed in line in a valley between the mountain proper and a high point of mountain that seemed to jut down between Missionary Ridge and the river. We moved forward up the mountain, but the Federals were already there; they had beaten us to the position. We fell back and took position on the main range, and formed a line with the left of our brigade resting over the tunnel already referred to, and extending along the mountain to the right, with Douglas' Texas Battery of twelve Napoleon guns in the center, and about 700 yards air line from the Federal battery on the point of the mountain already named.

It was now dark, the night is cold and crisp, and being so close to the enemy, we could have no fires and we had to just grin and bear it.

As soon as the first streak of daylight began to paint the east, the crack of the skirmishers' rifles in our front rang out, and they sounded as loud as cannon. Capt. Rhodes Fisher was again in command of the skirmishers, and he and Companies G of the 6th, 10th and 15th Texas regiments done their whole duty; during the night we threw up temporary works, such as we could make of old logs, loose rocks, etc., from where we were. Chattanooga was on an exact line between us and the point of Lookout mountain where Gen. Bragg's extreme left rested.

The morning of the 25th of November, 1863, was bright and frosty, yet there was a dense fog hovering about the top of Lookout mountain, but we could hear the roar of musketry and booming of cannon, and we knew that the Alabamians were having a tug at war with Hooker. They were fighting above the clouds. We could see the city and the valley. Long lines of infantry were moving up in our front. Now they are in range of our batteries, shot and shell were sent into their lines, they waver, but on they come. Cheatham's Tennessee division on a high mountain to our left sally out and drive the enemy in their front. But they rally and on they come in splendid order. Just now Maj.-Gen. Cleburne comes up on foot in rear of our line; he ordered the writer to take one company of the 3d and 5th Confederate and deploy them as skirmishers some forty yards down the mountain and in front of our line, and to remain until driven in by the enemy. We tipped our cap, formed the company and obeyed the command. We were immediately under our own guns, and when the artillery duel opened between the Douglas battery and the Federal battery on the high point just in our front, ours and our company of Irishmen's position was a noisy one, and very dangerous. The writer after getting the company deployed crouched down behind a very friendly chestnut tree. A big burly Irishman a few paces to our right said he was too busy to take a tree, when we reproached him for not protecting himself as much as possible. He was a fine soldier, the balls were flying fast, but he would stand out in a clear place, take deliberate aim and then watch to see the effect of his shot. Like all others of his race he was a wit. We had been there for some time; he finally with a twinkle about his eyes said, "Are you cold, Lieutenant?" We assured him that we were not. "Well," he said, "I didn't know, but thought ye were either cold or domed badly scared, from the way you're trembling and shaking." He was a splendid specimen of manhood. Just before sundown a shot broke his neck and he fell dead not ten feet from where the conversation occurred in the morning. Pat Kane went up from Missonary Ridge. He said during our conversation in the morning that if Jeff Davis would feed him and let him play cards all he wanted to, and furnish him a fight now and then, that he wouldn't care if the war lasted forty years. But we must pass along. On they came and ran us in. We thought our Irishman never would run, and we were ashamed to give the command to fall back on the main line. About 10 o'clock we were run in and then our whole line sallied out and drove the enemy back. Bragg's line, it will be remembered, was a semi-circle; Grant's army was inside the circle, therefore he could mass troops on any point of the line in less time than Bragg could, because Bragg's troops had to go around outside of the circle, giving Grant much the advantage in maneuvering his army and which he turned to good account. About 2 a. m. the fighting seem to be general all along the line. Some two hundred yards in our front, and near the Chattanooga end of the tunnel, there stood a dwelling, barn and some other outhouses, and right in the heat of the battle three or four women came out and passed through our line. They did not seem to be alarmed nearly as much as we have seen a Texas woman get at a mouse. About 4 p. m. Grant seemed to be concentrating his whole army on Cleburne's front. On they came line after line; we remember one brigade that had a green flag; they got up to within forty yards of our line. Things were getting pretty blue all around there. Gen. Cleburne came up on foot just in rear of our brigade and said in a very quiet sort of way: "Boys, take them in." That was enough. We sailed into them, captured many prisoners, six stands of colors, and lots of guidons. The writer had unbuckled his sword, and as we went over the works left it, grabbed a rock and went in. A good many of the Yankees played dead that had not been touched. The writer captured a whole company that had taken shelter behind a big chestnut log; they were more than willing to surrender.

Our regiment fought the 26th Missouri; we learned this from the wounded left on the field. We thought we had gained the day when the truth of the matter was we had broke their line just the length of our brigade. Some of us were very much annoyed at a general charge not being ordered, as the enemy in our front were running like wild cattle. Merritt Mathews, of Denton County, Chris Gose, of Wise County, and the writer and several others lit out after them on our own hook, and must have gone three hundred yards inside of their lines, when all at once we discovered a full line of Federal infantry, not more than forty yards to our right. They turned loose on us, but we all made it out. Gose was shot in the back, but the ball struck where his two blankets, rolled up and worn like a shot pouch, crossed. The blankets saved his life. A brass button turned a ball that struck Maj. Sanders square in the breast; it broke his right arm. In this charge Capt. Bill Shannon, of Parker County, with about twenty of his company captured two hundred Federals in the houses already referred to. Jim Shaw, of Waco, was in the charge and if we quote correct, he and a Federal soldier fought a duel.

Shaw was too quick for him, and got in his work. After this everything was very quiet, and we thought we had gained a great victory, and it was very natural, for we had cleaned up everything that came against us that day in the charge. Gen. Smith and Col. Mills, commanding the 6th, 10th and 15th Texas consolidated regiments, were wounded, and the command of the brigade fell on Col. Hiram B. Granbury, of the 7th Texas infantry.

Some time after nightfall, Col. Granbury ordered Capt. J. L. Leonard to take four companies and deploy them as skirmishers in front of our brigade, with orders to remain out until driven in. He had the writer detailed to act as adjutant, and the above orders was the first hint we had of things not being all right. The line of skirmishers was deployed about one hundred and fifty yards in advance of the line we had held all day.

About us and in rear of our line the dead and wounded were thick on the ground. We learned from the wounded that we had been fighting Missouri troops, especially the 26th Missouri infantry. Lieut. Burris, of Company B, 15th Texas infantry, now of McKinney,

Texas, was personally acquainted with several of them. We rendered such assistance as we could to the wounded.

By 8 o'clock quiet prevailed in the valley of Chattanooga, the pale moon looked down into the faces of many Confederates and Federals whose life blood had baptized the hills and valleys in a cause which each thought was in the right; but enough of this.

## CHAPTER XXII.

RETREAT FROM MISSIONARY RIDGE — WADE CHICKAMAUGA WHILE DIAMONDS OF FROST ARE FALLING — BATTLE OF RINGGOLD GAP.

At the close of the preceding chapter we bade the reader good-night while we were yet on picket duty after the great battle of Missionary Ridge, and during the few hours we were waiting and watching, we witnessed more of the horrors of cruel war. Near where we were standing on the line of skirmishers, a wounded Federal was sitting on the ground with his back against a tree, he had been shot through the bowels. He seemed to be a very intelligent young man and spoke of the certainty of having to die very soon in a very quiet, dignified manner. He belonged to the 26th Missouri infantry. Another young man of powerful build, and we suppose from the same regiment, had been seriously wounded in the head; he was some distance higher up the mountain than the one already named. He would rise to his feet and then fall face foremost down the mountain, uttering cries and groans that pierced the hearts of old soldiers. We thought at first that it was a ruse he was playing to get through our line, but upon examination we found he was seriously wounded and was as crazy as a "march hare." But those surroundings were tame to our feelings compared to the effect of the huzza, huzza, huzza, that commenced in the Federal lines to our left, and died away, away down yonder toward the base of Lookout mountain. "What does all this mean" was the question asked in low tones one of another. I cannot tell, there is some mistake, I thought we had gained a great victory. Anyway we have the satisfaction and the glory of mopping up the ground with everything that has come against we Texas and Arkansaw fellows to-day, we will wait and see what we will see. About 11 o'clock the order was passed down the line in a whisper, from post to post, for us to move out by the left flank, and to be careful as to making any sort of noise, not to allow saber or gun to strike with canteens, and not to tread on any sticks that might break and make a noise. We were old soldiers enough by this time to know what all this meant. We knew that the day had been lost, and in less time than it requires to pen one of these lines, such thoughts as these passed through our minds in rapid succession: if we can't hold such a line as this against those blasted Federals, where is the line or position between here and the coast of Georgia that we can hold? But enough of this. We moved out as quietly as if there had been but one man only. Up, over the mountain and down through a deep gorge, wrapped in deep darkness inside and outside. Not a word being uttered. The writer, along with Capt. Jack Leonard was marching at the head of the column, and if our memory is not out of joint, the first words spoken was the following little speech made by the writer to Capt. Leonard. "This, Captain, is the death-knell of the Confederacy, for if we cannot cope with those fellows over the way with the advantages we have on this line, there is not a line between here and the Atlantic ocean where we can stop them." He replied by saying, "Hush, Lieutenant, that is treason you are talking." Doubtless such expressions in the presence of the men might have been wrong, but we thought it all right as between officers. Captain Leonard was a patriot and a good soldier; he has passed over the river, and into that good country where there is no change in government rulers, and where wars, earthquakes, famines and pestilence never come. Peace to his ashes. We loved him like a brother.

On we go; pretty soon we come to where our division is camped in a sort of straggling, irregular manner in a great woodland. We laid down and rested an hour or two. The night was quite pleasant; some time before daylight we were up and put on the move, and about sunrise we arrived at Chickamauga station. This was on the Atlantic & Great Western Railway, and had been General Bragg's main depot of supplies. Here we began to see and realize the situation and learn something of how the battle had gone. There were thousands of bushels of shelled corn, corn meal and some bacon scattered around the station. We were halted, built fires and were broiling our bacon for breakfast. Off to our right, when facing Chattanooga, was a fort. We noticed some stragglers craning their necks over the parapets of the fort and looking in the direction the enemy would come, and we looked down that way too, and not more than three hundred yards from us a line of Federal cavalry formed across the railroad; their horses looked to be about sixteen feet high and each rider looked a regular Goliath, while the moral of Cleburne's division of Arkansaw, Texas and Mississippi troops was not the best in the world, yet it was the best in the army of Tennessee. Fact of the business is, every other division in the army was on a dead run for any place to get out of the reach of the Yankees. But to return. We did not stand on the order of our going but moved out at once. All day of the 26th and until late at night we were kept well in hand and on the move. About 11 o'clock at night we stopped on the banks of Chickamauga, near Ringold, Georgia, and oh, how tired and sleepy we were. We laid down and were asleep immediately. About 4 o'clock on the morning of the 27th, we were awakened and ordered into line. By this time it was cold and frosty; the moon was bright and clear, and seemed to cast an extra sheen of bright light over everything. We could even see the diamonds of frost as they fell through the cold, crispy air.

There were no boats nor bridges on which we could cross the Chickamauga creek, a creek it seemed we would never get away from, and we had to wade it. It was about thirty yards wide, and just deep enough to cut the average Confederate off in the neighborhood of his watch pocket. Some of the boys shed all their linen but their shirts, and sailed into it, while others went in like horses, with all their rigging on; the former fared better, even if we did have to climb the wet frozen banks with bare feet. But we felt quite snug after getting our clothes on and moving off, and having put that cold and turbulent stream between us and the enemy.

On we go down through the little town of Ringold. Ringold is located in a valley, locked in by mountains on the south, east and northeast. The dirt road and railroad approached the town from the east through a narrow gorge, cut through the mountain by " our Chickamauga creek." Gen. Bragg had sent orders to Gen. Cleburne to hold this gap until 12 o'clock if possible, and that if he could do so, he could save the army of Tennessee. Our line was formed two hundred yards up the side of the mountain and in the shape of the Roman letter

"V." Douglas' Texas battery was massed in the cut near the apex of the "V." Just about sunup came the Federals in high glee, down through town, banners flying, drums beating, with heads up and tails over the dash-board sort of way, as if they had nothing to do now but march right along through the country and pick up straggling rebels. "On they come in four lines, marching by the flank, right up to within seventy-five or a hundred yards of our hidden battery, when all at once, the pine tops with which our battery is covered are thrown off, and six twelve-pound Napoleon guns pour shot and shell into their ranks. They were utterly astonished and broke in great confusion, seeking shelter anywhere, behind dwellings, barns, outhouses, railroad embankment or anything else. But they were between the two wings of Cleburne's lines and we gave it to them good. We held the line until 1 o'clock and then retreated wading our Chickamauga creek again for the last time. The Federal loss was fearful, ours was light. The Confederate Congress voted the Texas brigade a resolution of thanks for its splendid conduct on this occasion, and besides, it made Col. H. B. Granbury, of the 7th Texas

Infantry, a Brigadier-General in the C. S. A. We fell back about a couple of miles and formed another line. The Federals came to where they could see us, but they did not want any more. We had put a taste in their mouths that ended the campaign. Late in the evening we moved on, marching quite all night. It may sound strange, but is true, that many of our men had lost so much sleep and were so nearly worn out, that they would go to sleep walking along and fall as suddenly as if they had been shot dead. Some time in the early morning of November 27, we arrived at Tunnel Hill, and took a position on a high range of hills south of town. The Yankees were satisfied to let us alone, and Gen. Bragg seemed satisfied with being let alone. Here we went into winter quarters.

## CHAPTER XXIII.

THE WINTER OF '63 AND '64 AT TUNNEL HILL, GEORGIA — VISIT TO MISS MARY A. H. GAY, DECATUR, GEORGIA — GEO. DEAN AND THE QUARTER OF BEEF—MISS LOU ANNIE RODGERS.

There is quite a difference in the appearance of the winter quarters of an army of volunteers, where every man or mess is left to be the sole judge of size, kind and quality of the houses they will build, and those of the regular army, where the whole matter is under the management of a quartermaster, skilled workmen and a civil engineer. In our winter quarters there was as great a variety of architecture as there is to be found in any city or town in the country. The thrifty, industrious soldier puts up a nice house, his style of architecture is good, everything about his premises looks tidy, and everything is kept in its place. While the lazy, shiftless soldier throws up most any sort of pen out of odds and ends that he can pick up here and there, and his larder and outfit for housekeeping is about on the same line, and if his quarters are not inspected every day or two by the officer of the day, he will allow it to get as filthy as a pig pen. In the army, as in civil life, our observations lead us to remark that, " the fittest survive." In other words, the soldier who takes good care of himself, and is watchful and industrious, generally gets enough to eat and is seldom sick, and possesses the powers of endurance. It requires an industrious, temperate man to make a successful soldier. But enough of this philosophy.

In a week or so, we were all tucked away in some sort of style, then commenced the routine of camp duty. While we were not in the immediate presence of the enemy, yet the danger of surprise was as great, and our line of pickets was as strong as at Chattanooga, and was placed some mile and a half in front of our main line across the creek. Don't know whether it was Chickamauga or not, anyway it was a very clever stream and we had to cross it on foot-logs or wade it. The month of December, 1863, and that of January, 1864, were hard and frosty; while on picket we were required to keep on all our clothing and accoutrements, and while we were permitted to have some fires near the line, yet our suffering from cold was great.

Did you ever lay down on that line with all your rigging on, with your feet to the fire, with the cape of a great overcoat you had captured from the Yankees pulled up over your head, and about the time you would sail off into a good snooze, about twenty-nine big body lice commence prizing up Hades down about your hips or between your shoulder blades, or away somewhere where you could not scratch without getting up and saying a good many unladylike words? We have experienced it. But every cloud has a silver lining, and we never have struck that condition in life where we couldn't see some sunshine; and we did here, even on this picket line. Just a little way out in front of our line, on what we called the neutral lands there lived a tanner by the name of Rodgers, and he had two daughters, Miss Kate and Miss Lou Annie, and they were bouncing, booming north Georgia mountain girls, honest, kind-hearted and as pure as snow-flake. The writer and Capt. Jack Leonard were not long in locating them. Capt. Leonard filed on Miss Kate and the writer laid claim to Miss Lou Annie, and in our "mind's eye," we can see her yet, tall, willowy, peach bloom in her cheeks, melting blue eyes, flaxen hair, cherry lips and teeth of pearl, and many the time have we crawled on our hands and knees on the snow and ice, to get through our picket lines to spend a long winter evening at her clever home; and our heart was exceedingly full of great sorrow, and we were sick nigh unto death when the commanding general said we must leave those regions and go "furder" back in Georgia. While here we lived pretty well, as all the territory between ours and the Federal lines was common foraging grounds. We remember a party of five going out on the hunt for meat. We will not say that we were with them, but the party consisted of George Dean, Bill Priddy, Walter Brandon and Newt Millhallon, all of Company "B" 15th Texas. The outfit succeed in capturing and killing a five year old steer. About the time it was dressed a party of Arkansaw boys came along and we divided with them. The layout then started for camps, our party taking it time about carrying a hind quarter by wearing it like a hunter does a bird bag or shot pouch. It was night-time, and when we struck the creek it was George Dean's time to carry it; he put it on, and started to walk the foot log, he fell in the creek and we thought for some minutes that we would not only lose the quarters of fat beef but that Dean would drown; but he held on to it, and made it to the banks. During the month of December desertions were frequent, but this was pretty well stopped when Gen. J. E. Johnston was put in command, about January 1st, 1864. His presence, improvement in rations, clothing, and the change in the routine of duty seemed to at once inspire the whole army with new and strong confidence. The boys under Johnston seemed to think every thing was all right, they went right along smoking their home-made pipes and playing poker and seemed as jolly as if out on a lark. Some time during the month of December, Capt. Jack Leonard received a letter from Miss Mary A. H. Gay, of Decatur, Ga., proposing that if he and the writer would visit her, she would present each with a pair of new Wellington boots. We had already been introduced to this excellent lady, and had been corresponding with her, because of letters of recommendation sent her by her half brother, Lieut. Stokes of the 10th Texas infantry. Of course we secured furloughs and went to see her during Christmas week. Miss Mary gave the writer her special attention, while her half sister, Miss Missouri Stokes, directed her attentions to Capt. Jack Leonard. Capt. Leonard was a master of the violin, and Miss Missouri had the scope of one of Chickerings best down very fine, and to say we two reveled in music and the company of these highly educated and excellent ladies, and filled up on ham and eggs, fried chicken, Lincoln coffee, cow butter and hot biscuits and slept on fat feather beds with our Napoleon heads resting on downy pillows, would be putting it tersely, truthfully and tamely. We want to carry the recollection of this Christmas week with us when we go over the River. We were wild young men then many miles from home, and doubtless our association with these accomplished women trimmed off many rough corners, and made impressions that have been factors in moulding some good trait in our characters. Doubtless many of our readers can call to mind Miss Mary A. H. Gay; she was an intimate friend of Miss L. Virginia

French, and a writer of prose and poetry, of acknowledged ability; but this was too rich for soldier's blood and too good to last. After one week we returned to our command at Tunnel Hill and to our rations of blue Florida beef, corn bread and molasses.

Some time during the month of February, our division was shipped by railroad via Atlanta, West Point to Montgomery, Alabama. We were rushed off down there to head off that big raid the Federals made from Memphis, into Mississippi, when the city of Meridian was burned. We got as far as Montgomery only, and were shipped back next day. It seems that Gen. Sherman at Chattanooga, was not long in finding that Gen. Johnston had weakened his forces by sending our division off, and commenced an advance on our lines at once, hence our return. On this trip we boys had whole gobs of fun. We would write notes as the cars run, tie them to sticks, rocks or anything else so that we could throw them to every girl we saw, and the result was each of us secured a sweetheart correspondent in Georgia or Alabama, and some kept up the correspondence long after " Grim-visaged war had smoothed his wrinkled front." The writer had two on his string, Miss Rebecca Savage, of Savage Station, Ga., and Miss Mollie E. Harris, of Auburn, Alabama. We never met either of them, but from the description they gave of themselves they were pretty and no doubt right sweet, and the style and subject-matter of their letters assured us that we had our hands full if we coped with them successfully in writing readable letters.

Gen. Sherman's forces returned to their lines around Chattanooga, and we went into camps about two miles north of Dalton, and remained there until the 2d of May, when the campaign opened that resulted in Sherman's march to the sea.

## CHAPTER XXIV.

GRANBURY'S AND LOWERY'S BRIGADE FIGHT A BATTLE WITH SNOWBALLS — A FURLOUGH — GOOD TIME IN GEORGIA — THE GEORGIA CAMPAIGN OPENS.

About the first of March there fell a big snow. The following happening so impressed it on the writer's mind that he will doubtless always remember it.

Gen. Lowery's Mississippi brigade was camped just a little ways over north of us. Granbury's brigade of Texans attacked them for a battle with snowballs. We charged right up to their dog tents. We were in a very aggressive squad. A big, red-headed freckled-face Mississippian captured and carried us quite a distance on his shoulders inside of their lines, and when he turned us loose we made a break for our own line, and one of our men hit us in the left eye with a big half ice and half snow ball, and laid one Confederate out. We were carried into Col. Abercombie's tent and were so blind when the battle was over that we had to be led back to our quarters. We cannot see well out of that eye to this day. Another circumstance during the morning was the shooting of a deserter. We were marched out while the snow was falling thick and fast, and formed into three sides of a square. The condemned man was sitting on his coffin facing a platoon of soldiers under command of a lieutenant. They were about twenty paces from him, and at the command "Ready, take aim, fire!" he fell forward dead. The contrast between the dark, gloomy, condemned man, the black coffin he was sitting on, and the white, whirling, whispering snow-flakes as they came from above, was indeed striking. The whole thing viewed from one stand-point suggested to the mind of a man of a charitable cast of mind, that our boasted civilization is but a little ways ahead of the heathen, but when viewed from the stand-point of sound policy and moral obligations, the man that will desert his country, his army, and betray his kith and kin and go to the enemy, deserves death.

About the 1st of April the writer succeeded in getting a thirty days' furlough. and no young man ever felt prouder of license authorizing some authority to make him and the woman of his choice partners in all things for life, than we did this leave of absence. Along with it was an order for transportation in kind, and we were soon on board the cars bound for Georgia. We made our way to the little city of Decatur, and from a Doctor Maddox and Miss Mary A. H. Gay, we secured letters of marque and reprisal to sail into the neighborhood of their friends and connection near Madisonville, Ga., a fine rich old country, over in the northeastern part of the State, where few soldiers had been, and to say that we had a royal good time at the princely homes of those old cotton planters is the best English we can command at this moment. We stopped first with a Mr. Stovall, and from his house as headquarters or base of operations, we made frequent raids into the surrounding country, from one to twenty-five miles, attending picnics, fishing parties and balls. We were dressed in a common suit of Georgia jeans, with one side of our hat pinned up with a five point silver star, and as a young man with two good strong arms and a pair of good legs was a rare thing to be seen in that part of the Empire State.

The young ladies, bless their sweet souls, vied with each other in paying us nice attentions, and we were just vain enough to be led off by our vanity into the belief that our good looks and soldierly appearance was the card that was winning all. We look back now and see that they poked lots of good-natured fun at us, and all was not gold that glittered. A special invitation was sent us to attend a fish fry picnic and boat ride, some twenty miles away in a settlement known as the Hamilton Bugg neighborhood. Mr. Stovall furnished us transportation and we took it in. Here we met an army of pretty girls, refugees from East Tennessee, South Carolina, Virginia and North Carolina. Here our good legs, strong arms and Texas star made us the lion of the occasion as we thought. The picnic was on the banks of a beautiful, clear river at a big spinning factory, a few miles from a little town on the railroad called Maxey Station. After eating, fishing, talking, courting, flirting to our heart's content, a motion prevailed that we adjourn to the Masonic Hall near by and spend the remainder of the day in tripping "the light fantastic toe." The hall was soon put in order and we went in. We have traveled in many States since that time, and have seen crowds of pretty women in New York, St. Louis, New Orleans and our own great Texas, but the impression that these girls, as they were sitting in rows on the four sides of that great hall, were the prettiest lot of women that we have ever seen, has not been altogether removed, and as the writer was the only young man there who had a pair of good legs, they almost danced us to death. Those pretty girls would engage us for a dozen sets ahead. To put it plainly, we were in sweetness up to our eyes, and they danced us until an old gentleman, a looker-on, whispered in our ear that they were putting up a job on us and intended to dance us until our tongue hung out like a choked 'possum. We took the hint and hid out. We remember him kindly, for if he had not given us the word, there is no telling what might have happened.

While in this neighborhood our headquarters were at Mr. Hamilton Bugg's. We carry with us recollections of the kind, motherly treatment of his good wife and the nice time we had with his daughter Mattie. I see her yet, a pretty, blue-eyed, rosy-cheeked, kind-hearted girl, but doubtless, a quarter of a century having swept by, has put crow's feet about her eyes and "silver threads amongst the gold." Yes, we remember so well Miss Hattie and Julia Cochran, the former, with her black curls, sparkling black eyes, and the latter a beautiful blonde. But thirty days' running in such clover go by like a dream in the night, a tale already told, and back to our command we must go.

When we got to the army, May 7th, 1864, the great Georgia campaign had already commenced. We found our brigade in line of battle, about one mile north of Resacca, Georgia. We reported to Col. Garland, commanding our regiment at the time. Our Company, "B," was out on the skirmish line, and he suggested that we remain at his headquarters until it came in. Being anxious to see the boys, we obtained permission to go out to where they were. Armed with a bright new cavalry saber, we started out. Our line of battle was on a range of hills running quite north and south; at the base of the hill a field set in, taking in the valley. The Federal line was in the thick woodland about 400 yards across the field. We made our way down to the left of the company and found Newt Millhollon and one of the other boys and told them all about the fun we had seen, and then started across to the right to where our old schoolmate, Lieut. Sam Beck, was. Millhollon insisted that it was a dangerous undertaking, for the reason the Federals had a battery just across the field and would shoot. We went along though anyhow, hacking the pine brush with our big sword very leisurely, and when about the center of our line, the Federals turned loose a big cannon, the ball passing about two yards in front of us and tearing a hole in the side of the hill large enough to bury an ox. We were not to say alarmed but felt exceedingly lonesome. We could not afford to run because we had acted foolhardily, and were foolhardy enough to carry it out. We walked on and to all appearances just as leisurely as before, and about the time we got on the line of the shot, they sent another one just in behind us. We could feel the wind from it. We passed along at a great effort and soon found our friend Beck. We were so shocked when we got to where he was that we sank down feeling thankful that we were alive, but were exhausted; Lieut. Beck remarked that he was a good doctor on such an occasion and reached us an extra canteen that he had swung around his neck, and to our exceeding great joy it was full of good whisky. The boys had raided somebody's headquarters the night our army left Dalton, and found a barrel of whisky, and all hands filled their canteens. We have never struck the article before nor since when it came in better time and tasted half so good. It was not long before we felt like we could whip ten to one.

On the morning of the 8th while it was yet dark, our division moved down and took up a position just in front of a fort and near the railroad bridge across Etawa river. The morning was very foggy, and while we were marching by the flank to our position, the Federals fired on us. We could hear the balls strike our men; it was here Pink Roberson of Wise County, lost a leg, and J. P. Fullingim, of the same county his sight eye.

On the morning of the 9th while it was yet dark, our division crossed the river on a muffled pontoon bridge, and we knew by this that the artillery and the army were ahead of us. Our next line was formed about 10 o'clock, near a little town called Calhoun. Late in the afternoon our line was put in motion, and the next line we formed was near a clever little city called Kingston. Here we remained in line of battle all night.

## CHAPTER XXV.

### THE TERRIFIC BATTLE OF NEWHOPE CHURCH, GEORGIA, MAY 27, 1864.

On the 12th we passed through Kingston, Ga., and camped in a rough hilly country, between the above named town and Cartersville. On the morning of the 13th we were called in line and Gen. Johnston's much discussed battle order was read. From the tone of the order it seemed that we had reached the point where the General commanding proposed to give battle. The boys seemed more delighted at the prospect of our rounding up and giving the Yankees a fight, than alarmed at the prospect of their lives being put in peril. All extra baggage was disposed of, the boys tightened their belts, and at the command loaded their guns carefully. We moved forward in line of battle quite a mile, halted and remained there until about 3 o'clock in the afternoon, when we were moved off in the direction of Atlanta. We formed another line near Cartersville, and remained there until quite daylight on the morning of the 14th, and while the cocks (and there seemed to be a thousand of them in the little city) were crowing their throats raw in their efforts to apprise those of the city who were in nice, clean beds, of the fact that the God of Day was sending up signals in the east, warning all of his approach, we passed through the city as cheerful and as jolly a body of soldiers as ever walked God's foot-stool under similar circumstances. About noon we crossed the river and went into camps on the banks of the laughing, clear and sparkling waters of Pumpkin Vine creek. Here we remained until the 22nd, putting in the time very nicely in bathing in the limpid waters of Pumpkin Vine.

On the 22nd the whole army seemed to be on the move off, on a line at right angles to the Atlantic & Western Railroad, and in the direction of Powder Springs and Dallas. We marched two days in this direction and on the 25th we were marched back over the same road and were put in line of battle east of Newhope Church. While here the writer had occasion to visit Ector's Texas brigade. It was in line of battle, its skirmishers were having a pretty warm fight with those of the enemy. We went out onto the line and found our old-time friend, Capt. Sam Lusk. Something had gone wrong and he was swearing like a Norwegian sailor.

On the morning of the 27th, Granbury's brigade was in position on the extreme right of the army; our line was on a ridge; in our front was quite a farm, the farmhouse was empty, and the family before leaving seemed to have made some effort to store away in safe places their household goods. We found a feather bed and several other articles in an old well. All this time away to our left the booming of cannon and the roar of small arms could be heard. About 4 p. m. a courier dashed up to Granbury's headquarters under a great oak, and handed him a dispatch. The General did not wait to send orders to the commanders of regiments to get their regiments ready to move but rose up at once and gave the command: "Attention, Brigade!" We were in line, every man in his place, in less time than it requires to pencil four of these lines, and at the command "Right face! forward! double quick march!" we were off on a run. We were moved to the right about the length of our brigade, came to a halt, and the command for the men to put caps on their guns was given. We were in a big road; opposite the left of our brigade was the corner of the farm already referred to. Near the fence a deep gorge set in running east and about the length of our brigade, and spread out in a valley farm at the foot of the gorge. Between the two farms was a heavy woodland. We moved some forty yards down the hill in the thick brush, and as we went in a line of Confederate cavalry moved out. We were commanded to lay down, and by this time a strong line of Federal infantry struck us. It was an open field fight. The enemy, so the prisoners we captured said, thought we were only a thin line of cavalry, and they came at us with a vim based upon that mistaken idea. Line after line they came against us. Their lines were so much longer than ours they extended into the field to our right, and about one hour by sun they had passed through the field and were several hundred yards in the rear of our right. General Granbury sent his Adjutant-General, the gallant Capt. Jose T. Hearne, to lead the 8th Arkansas of Gen. Govan's brigade in a charge to drive them back. He succeeded, but was shot dead just as he was entering the old field. Just at sundown the order came down the line from mouth to ear, "Fix bayonets!" In an instant a thousand bayonets gleamed in the twilight, and every man seemed determined to hold this line or give up his life in the effort. Just before dark the command came down the line "Cease firing!" No one could tell who gave it, but it was obeyed. At this the Federal line rose up in our front, not more than fifteen yards from us. We commanded them to surrender. A few of them threw down their arms and came in. This it seems was a ruse to fool us and afford the enemy time to get their line in order, as the bluff they had to come up was very steep, and difficult to climb in line of battle. When it was about quite dark, and they thought they had lines enough and force enough to run over us, an officer stepped to the front and said, "Run over them, men!" This uncovered to us the ruse they had been playing and we poured a volley into them that completely routed them. They fell back down to the bottom of the gorge, which was about one hundred yards from our line. Gen. Granbury knew that we could not live in peace with them at such close range, and sent Capt. Dick English to Gen. Cleburne's headquarters asking permission to charge them. Gen. Cleburne replied that he could not give his permission for the move, but that he would refer the matter at once to army headquarters, and that in the meantime Gen. Granbury should be governed by his own best judgment as to what was best to be done under existing circumstances. This was enough for the lion-hearted Granbury, and about 1 o'clock in the morning we were very quietly formed in line, every man being fully advised as to what was to be done, and at the sound of the bugle we dashed down with a yell, into that dark gorge, like a whirlwind. This was just a little too much for the Federals; they broke and in their efforts to get away they tore the brush like cattle. Next morning we could locate where their lines had been by the guns they had run off and left. Well, it was enough to scare them, we yelled like mad men as we were, and if they had stood their ground it would have been a hand to hand fight. Down in this gorge it was as dark as a pile of black cats, and we got pretty badly mixed and done some fighting amongst ourselves.

We could hear all up and down that deep gorge such challenges as, "Who's that?" "Who are you?" Pop! pop! "I belong to the 167 New York, or 144 Illinois." "Well, come into my shuck, ye greasy flitter." We captured about two hundred of them and when the sun had chased the shades of night away beyond the Rocky Mountains, it revealed a scene on that hillside that was sickening to look upon. All along in front of the center and left of our brigade the ground was literally covered with dead men. To look upon this and then the beautiful wildwoods, the pretty flowers as they drank in the morning dew, and listen to the sweet notes of the songsters in God's first temples, we were constrained to say, "What is man and his destiny, what a strange thing is the problem of life." We dug two pits and in them deposited the mortal remains of about five hundred men. During the day Johnson and quite all the general officers of the army visited and inspected the battle grounds, and all agreed that they had never seen or read of anything like it.

Our brigade was armed with a little short gun, called the Belgian Rifle, and they sent a ball with such force that the undergrowth and small trees in our front that measured from two to five inches and over were actually shot into shreds.

About two o'clock in the afternoon we were moved out and to the right. We remember passing just in rear of our line where some half dozen dead comrades were lying on the green grass in the cool shade of a sugar tree, and they looked so quiet, when all around was in such terrific strife, that we almost wished that we were with them. After going about a mile we were put in line and worked all day digging rifle pits, which were abandoned about dark, and after marching all night we went into position on what was called the Pine Mountain or Golgotha Church line.

## CHAPTER XXVI.

PINE MOUNTAIN—GEN. LEONIDAS POLK KILLED—SLEEP IN WATER HALF SIDE DEEP—THE KENESAW LINE—JOHNSTON REMOVED, HOOD APPOINTED IN HIS STEAD.

When we left our readers in last chapter, we were on our way to Pine Mountain or the Golgotha Church line. The night was very dark. The whole army seemed to be moving on one road. All night long it was moved a few paces and then stand and wait. We were so tired and sleepy that strong men would give up and fall down in the mud or drop out to one side and it seemed that they would be sound asleep by the time they would get laid down.

About daylight our brigade was strung out in line just across the creek and east of Golgotha. The church house was an old-fashioned building, and was the place where the Missionary Baptists of that section met each Lord's day to worship. We remained here from the 2d to the 18th of June. It was on this line that the great bishop of the Episcopal church and general in the army, Leonidas Polk, was killed. The news of his death passed down our line from man to man. The circumstances of his death as we gathered them at the time, were as follows: Generals Johnston, Hardee and Polk had gone to the front on Pine Mountain. The enemy discovered them and opened fire with a battery. Johnston and Hardee remarked that it was an unsafe place. Gen. Polk remained and was struck by a cannon ball. He was a great and good man and when leading his corps in battle he wouldn't swear, but would say to his men, " Give it to them, boys, like General Cheatham says." The only command General Cheatham gave was " Give them h—l boys."

While it was yet dark we moved out on the morning of the 18th, and formed a line on a high range of hills. Here during the forenoon we were under the most terrific fire from field artillery we remember being subject to during the war.

We remember seeing Brig.-Gen. Polk of North Carolina, as he was carried from the field, he having been wounded in the leg by a piece of shell. All day we remained on this line, and how the rain did pour down on us all day, only those that were there can tell. We remember when night came of trying to sleep in water half side deep. The undertaking was all right until we would move and let in a lot of cold fresh water, then sleep would quit our eyes, and slumber flee from our eyelids. We had the consolation, however, of knowing that each of us were drowning several hundred " gray backs."

About midnight we were put on the move and went into position about sunrise on the great Kenesaw line. The writer's company was amongst those put on picket. We marched deployed as skirmishers quite a mile, through a field of growing oats, and the slow rain that had been falling all night made the trip through this field very much like wading a river. About ten o'clock we were ordered back to where we had first formed in the morning, the right of our company resting at the Cartersville and Marietta road, while the left extended out into an old field. In a very short time we had breastworks made of rails, old logs, etc., that afforded some protection. By eleven o'clock the enemy was pressing us, and they seemed to be getting bolder and more aggressive every day, while we from the effects of so many times giving up lines and falling back were getting more or less out of hope and timid. There fell several hard rains during the day and on some parts of our line the men at times were in water up to their arm-pits. Between these showers a constant firing was kept up, we doing all we could to hold the line, and the enemy trying to press us out. By sunset our lines were only a few paces apart. By this time the clouds had rolled away, the sun went down clear and left the big silver moon high in the heavens to give us light in our efforts to take each other's lives. About ten o'clock Lieut. J. L. McCracking, commanding Company "E" came out with his company to relieve us. The writer went back some twenty paces in rear of our line to show him how to deploy his company to cover the ground we were on. We pointed with our sword where his right should rest near the big road, and to a stump where his left must extend to; about this time a dark fleecy cloud that had been over the face of the moon passed off and a Federal who was very near our line took aim at the writer. He was a good shot, as the ball singed our mustache; the shock was so great we came very near falling. Merrett Matthews standing close by insisted that we were shot, declaring he heard the ball strike us. Another instance of narrow escape and we pass along. During the day a bomb shell exploded in a pile of rails and it was hard to tell for a few moments which were blown the highest, the rails, pieces of rails, or the boys; we remember Frank Cook of Wise County, as one of the boys who went up and came down running; he stopped, however, behind a big stump just a few paces in rear, he yet had his rifle in hand and went at them as though nothing had happened. He was a big light-haired, blue-eyed boy; we can see him yet as he deliberately lays his gun up by that old stump and takes aim. This closed our day's work of the 19th of June, 1864.

We were marched back to the main Kenesaw line, and after making a supper on cold " biled " Florida beef and cold, musty, wet, clammy corn bread, we turned in wrapped in wet blankets and the last sound that greeted our ears as we went to sleep and the first when we woke up in the morning was the voice of a minnie, not the Miss Minnie that used to play and sing for us over in Wise County, before grim-visaged War put on his paint, but minnie balls, and the variety of tunes they sung when passing over us night and day, seemed to take in the whole range and scope of the world's gamut of music. We were on this line just fourteen days and nights and the booming of cannon and keen crack of the rifles was kept up all day and night, except at such places along the line as the men would get up an armistice on their own hook. The redoubts for our brigade were about one hundred yards in front of our main line of works and the Federal line of the same kind was in some places as near as twenty yards of ours. When conditions were favorable, a Yankee soldier would step out and shake a newspaper and say, "Hello, Johnnie Reb." "Hello, Yank, what do you want." "Let's hold awhile, we want to swap some of our Lincoln coffee for yer' flat tobacco." "All right, lay down yer gun and meet us half way." Thus we would meet, crack jokes, swap rations of tobacco and coffee and have a jolly good time until some big officer of the day on either side would come along, then all hands would scamper back to their holes in the ground. These respites from constant watching and fighting were a great help to us.

We had now been on the march or in line of battle quite sixty days, and hard service with poor rations of corn bread, bean crackers and boiled beef was telling on the health of the army. Referring to the bean crackers any good soldier will stand by us in the assertion that after soaking it a day and night in water it would come out as tough as a cow's horn. Not having had a change of food or raiment for sixty days, we were not to say very clean, the scurvy broke out amongst us, some of the boys' legs were as black and brown as navy tobacco. Gen. Johnston had several car loads of tomatoes shipped up from Florida, Alabama and other States and as an antiscorbutic they proved a success, but the bodylice had a dead sinch on us, until some of the boys discovered that they could not stand smoke and heat. Just before turning in at night each fellow would rake him up a pile of dry leaves, set fire therein and hold his shirt over the smoke and heat, and the big, fat lice would drop into the fire and pop like popcorn popping in the skillet at home. If you never have tried it you know nothing of how confortable a shirt feels to a fellow after putting it through the above process; we would then crawl into the shirt and then into our dog tent and sleep as sweetly as a tom-cat stretched on a great rug before the fire-place at the old homestead. But we must move along.

'Tis sunset on Kenesaw, and from our line on the mountain we can see the beautiful city of Atlanta, the gate to the South, and only about twelve or fifteen miles away; and as we take in the situation after sixty days' hard fighting, the care-worn looks of the officers and men, the quiet manner of moving the heavy artillery to the rear, we wonder what is coming next, but almost as we expected, about 11 o'clock of the night of July the 3rd we were ordered to abandon the great Kenesaw line, and march through the pretty city of Marietta, the citizens of which seemed as quietly asleep in their beds as if an angel of peace was roosting in every shade tree.

On the morning of the 4th we formed another line near the Chattahouche river, and by the time we were ready for fight Sherman's advance was in sight. About one o'clock they charged our picket line and drove the men in. Capt. Rhodes Fisher, commanding our regiment, ordered Lieut.

Harroll, commanding Company A, and the writer, to take their companies and retake the line of picket works. The Federals were in our advance works and we had to go at them through an open space we had cleared ourselves in front of our main line, a distance of about two hundred yards. We all knew that there were but two things we could do, go into the works on them and be killed in the attempt, or refuse to go. We went at them like a herd of wild cattle; they gave us a warm reception but we made them pull their freight. About sundown they made an effort to retake the works but we repulsed them, a Federal Lieutenant was shot down, badly wounded near our line; he gave some of the boys his rings, watch and some other things and requested that they be sent to his wife and two children somewhere in Indiana, after the war closed. Some time during the night we were moved back and put on an already fortified line nearer the river. Here Sherman seemed to want to stop and rest a few days and spit on his hands, and God knows that we were more than willing, for we not only needed rest, but we wanted time to wash our shirts as well as take a swim in the Chattahouche.

On the 12th this scientifically fortified line was abandoned, we crossed over the river and lay around loose under the shades of the great oaks and rested until July the 18th; this was a bright Sunday and the boys instead of all going to hear preaching had their blankets spread and were playing draw-poker or shaking dice. The writer along with a majority of his company was playing a little game in the deep shade of a great oak, on a big moss-covered flat rock for a table, when Adjutant John Willingham came up and read the order from President Davis removing Gen. Jos. E. Johnston from command and putting Gen. John B. Hood in command of the Army of Tennessee. The boys all threw down their cards and collected in little groups discussing the new move they were all dissatisfied, but soon dismissed the whole with the remark h—l will break loose in Georgia sure enough now. Hood was a bull-dog fighter from away back, and President Davis could not have suited General Sherman better, had he commissioned him to have made the appointment.

## CHAPTER XXVII.

Gen. Hood goes on the war path — Battle of Peach Tree Creek, July 20, 1863 — Wounded by a Yankee bullet — In hospital at Forsythe — At the Rev. Cleveland's — A jolly good time after all.

Early on the morning of the 19th, Gen. Hood had the whole army on the move " right in front." We were old soldiers enough by this time to know that this order in our line of march meant that Sherman was making a move to turn our right flank. Our division was moved to and put on a line some two miles east of the Peach Tree Creek road. Here we remained overnight. On the morning of the 20th, we were moved still further to the right in the direction of Decatur. We remained here in line of battle until about 3 o'clock in the afternoon, when we were moved in double quick time back to the Peach Tree Creek road, and our division maned a line of works and at right angles to this road just in front of a big church house. The right center of

Granbury's Texas brigade, being near the road, with Govan's Arkansaw brigade, or Joshes', as we boys called them to our right. The writer was detailed and put in command of Company "C" Lieut. John W. Stewart of Grayson County, Texas, being too indisposed to go into battle with his company. Every movement pointed with the unerring finger of certainty to the fact that somebody was going to get badly hurt and that in short order.

In front of our brigade was an open field about four hundred yards across. About 4:30 o'clock the command was given, "forward march;" we quit the works and moved out into the field. The Federals greeted us with a terrific fire of shot and shells but as we were moving down the hill they passed over our heads, doing no damage except that of making a fellow feel like he was very small game to be shot at with such guns.

On we go, now the lines come to the fence on the farm already referred to, the line halts, and the men take hold of it and just bodily lift it from its foundation and throw it down; just at this moment a blinding flash right in our front and a shell explodes. It seemed to be filled with powder and ounce balls. It laid a good many of the boys out and among the number was Capt. Ben Tyus, and the writer. The former was wounded in the ankle, while the latter received an ounce ball in the upper third of his left thigh. As we fell we noticed that about two inches square of our gray Georgia jeans pants had gone in with the shot; this was conclusive that a piece of the shell had passed through our thigh and had necessarily cut the femoral artery, and that therefore we would be a dead Confederate in just three minutes, as our understanding is that the femoral artery cut would let all the blood in a man out in that time. However we made a grip on the wound with our right hand intending to stop the blood as much as possible and thereby hold on to life long enough to give our past history a hasty going over and to repeat all the prayers we knew. Four big stout fellows picked us up on a litter and started back to the line of breastworks. We had to pass through a galling fire of minnies, shot and shell; we were not alarmed at all at this, because our mind was made up to quit the earth, and we were now only waiting, as the saying goes, for death to strike us square in the face. We finally ventured to inquire of one of the men carrying us, "If we were bleeding much." He was a witty Irishman, and replied, "Not a drap of the rudy current to be seen, Lieutenant." These words brought back our hopes that had already gone over the hills out of sight, and made us remark that an improvement in gait would soon land us out of reach of these Yankee bullets, and then we chuckled in our sleeve when the thought occurred may be this wound will win a good furlough and if it does, won't we have fun with those Georgia girls. This may all sound like a strange line of thoughts to run through one's mind in so short a time and under such circumstances, but all this is sound common sense compared to some things we are guilty of doing during our natural lives. Pretty soon we were dumped over on the safe side of our earthworks, the field surgeon examined our wound and pronounced it an ugly one, but not necessarily fatal. We thanked him from the bottom of our heart for these words. About ten of us were piled into an old ambulance and the driver pulled out for Atlanta. We were landed at the City Hall, the commons around this building having been turned into a carving pen, and the doctors had more subjects than they had table room. We were laid on a big broad pine table and four stout men put to hold us, one to each arm and leg, while Doctors D. F. Stuart of Houston and C. Lipscomb of Denton, went into the ugly wound with probes and fingers in search for the missing piece of our Georgia jeans; chloroform was too scarce and costly to be used on us and besides there were so many needing attention that the doctors could not spare time to administer it except in very bad cases, therefore we had to endure the pain. The ball that struck us was mashed flat on one side to about the size of a quarter, and went in the flat way turning on the femoral artery. We were then stored away on a nice clean cot in a new tent in a little park just across the street in front of the Trout House, and remained there overnight and were shipped early next morning along with many others down to a little city on the Macon road called Forsythe. And now being away from our command we plead our lack of any knowledge as to what the boys were doing, as an excuse for devoting so much time to our personal experiences in a Confederate hospital, and to our raids over the country while on furlough. All the Texas fellows were located in an old two story hotel on the southeast corner of the square, chicken, good coffee, fresh butter and a clean bed here was rich fare, compared to what we had been having in the army. Capt. Ben Tyus, a young man from Memphis, Tenn., and the writer, were assigned to a room on the second floor and immediately over the office. We not only had a nice clean room, good beds and good grub, but the lady who was head boss of our ward was better than all these. She was so kind and attentive to our every want, that we were soon at war amongst ourselves about whose sweetheart she should be as soon as we got on crutches, but to our great astonishment the nearer well we got the less attention she paid to us, and by the time we were going around she didn't know us at all. How strange these women do sometimes act. But seriously, she was in the right, because if she had undertaken to listen to the love that all of us soldiers would have made to her, her time would have all been consumed and those needing attentions neglected. We were having what might be called a hog-killing time, until the break-bone wounded man's fever set up in this mortal coil. When our wound commenced suppurating, matter pressed on what the doctor called the femoral nerve, causing the most acute pain in our left arm and leg, the tender place in our knee and the sugar bone in our left arm were the points most affected; the pain was so great that we certainly would have had lock-jaw had we not been kept under the influence of morphine for 18 days and nights. The head surgeon, a doctor Patterson from Murphysboro, Tennessee, we remember very kindly, but that slick hat fellow from Memphis, was doubtless a good doctor but we owe him one if we ever meet up with him on this side of the river. Proud flesh formed in our wound, causing great pain and we were making lots of noise about it. The way it protruded from the big hole in our thighs made it look more like a big rank red rose at a certain distance from it than anything else we can compare it to. He sat us down one hot afternoon, on the side of our cot, and while a big Irishman by the name of Pat Bates from New Orleans held our arms behind us, he gouged in to the wound with the sharp corners of a chunk of bluestone, until he burned it as white as the paper we are writing on, it was a terrible ordeal to pass through, and when the Irishman turned us loose we struck the doctor one of the best blows we had ever struck with our fist, right on top of his slick nail keg hat, and drove it down on his head to his ears. He laughed and took it all good naturedly. The next falling out we had was when he suddenly cut off our supply of morphine. We lay wide awake four days and nights. We made so much noise about it that the doctor finally brought us a quart bottle of Confederate whisky. We threw it at him. We didn't know then that a couple or more good bumpers of it would cause sleep to come. From this time on we commenced to improve, and were soon able to go on crutches down to the regular dining-room.

About the first of September, a rich old Georgia planter by the name of Cleveland came in with his fine carriage and driver, and hauled Maj.-Gen. W. B. Bate of Tennessee, Lieut. McCracken and this scribe to his fine old plantation on the Chatahoochee. He was a hardshell Baptist preacher. We remained at his house about one month, and to say that we luxuriated on his old "peach" and candied honey therein, and fed on young pigeons, and the fat of the land would be telling a simple plain gospel truth. Gen. Bate was one of the best talkers we have ever met in life, and that old peach and honey kept his tongue oiled up to a queen's taste.

About October the first, we returned to the city. All this time Hood and Sherman had been shaking the country about Atlanta, Jonesboro and Lovejoy station with heavy ordnance and the tread of mighty armies. Everything was getting pretty squally about Forsythe and in all the country around, and because of the danger of Federal cavalry raids quite all the wounded and sick had been shipped to Macon and other points south. About 4 p. m., the last train coming out before the fall of Atlanta ran up to the station at Forsythe. It consisted of an engine, tender and one box car. This was the first but not the last ride we have had on a car when the throttle valve was being manipulated by a dead drunk engineer. The train came dashing up like a cannon ball. We climbed on top the box car, and like all other soldiers, had a habit of saying, "Here's your mule." An old fellow who was sitting a-straddle of a feather bed he had roped to the walking board, said: "Yes, if you ride this train you can claim to be two mules, for that d—m engineer is drunk." We sat down on the board and he pulled out. Pretty soon we were a-straddle of it, the next move we laid flat down on it and locked our legs and arms around it to hold on. It was about fifty miles to Macon, and the best estimate we could make of the time, we ran it in about thirty minutes. It seemed that the car we were on would jump about four feet from the track and run forty yards before coming down to its knitting again. When we arrived in Macon every box was smoking like a tar kiln; we had lost our cap and the wonder is that the hair and scalp did not go with it. We felt dazed and full of wind, and the natural taste of a drink of Georgia pine top whisky at the Brown house was the first thing convincing that us was certainly we.

From here we went down to the old city of Americus. Lieut. Jim Perry, of Byran, Texas, and a Doctor Smith, from New Orleans, and the writer had quarters in a room in the court house while here. We were all nice young men. The baskets of nice palatable provisions that the good women of the grand old town supplemented our regular rations with made our living very fine. We were having a royal time laying up in day time and chewing sugar-cane, and running around courting at night, until one day about the 11th' of November, a red-headed, red-whiskered, red-eyed doctor by the name of Redwine, came into our room and remarked in a very authoritive manner, "this outfit is about ready to go to the front." We knew he was about right, and asked for orders. Lieut. Perry because of a lame hand was made military conductor on a railroad. Dr. Smith took orders to his command, and the writer received orders to go to his command which was then at Florence, Ala., and was also instructed to gather up all the able-bodied men he could find at Columbus, Ga., Montgomery, Ala., Selma and Meridian, Miss. We had one hundred and five men on our roll. Among them was a very handsome, smart young fellow, from Memphis, by the name of Hyde, who had been a comedian in a theater there before the war. He could make fun for us all. We arrived at Corinth in the night-time. Hyde and the writer went to headquarters and drew rations for one hundred and five men, but when we went to our camping place, just outside the city, we had only five men to answer to roll-call. We had a quarter of fat beef and lots of crackers. The morning was cold and frosty, and when we awoke, got up and looked out over the country, the outlook was disheartening. Corinth was a hard, dirty-looking town, the few people remaining seemed to be out of humor with themselves and all of their kind. The country around had the appearance of having been blasted by the curse of the gods. After two days marching we reached our command at Florence, Ala., on November 19th, 1864.

## CHAPTER XXVIII.

HOOD'S CAMPAIGN IN TENNESSEE—THE SPRING HILL FAILURE—BATTLE OF FRANKLIN, NOVEMBER 30, 1864.

The army remained for some days camped around on the hills about Florence. This delay was for the purpose of drawing all the able-bodied men from the hospital, and also all that could with safety be spared from the forts, as well as to get supplies for the campaign into Tennessee. We were poorly clad, and as for arrangements for sleeping comfortably, that was out of the question. The writer and his bunk mate, Lt. Sam Beck, raked together a big pile of dried leaves for a feather bed, and until they wore out it was a pretty good substitute. Each of us had a hole in the ground just to fit our hip, and we changed from side to side at the word of command. In other words, we "spooned," and when we would get cold beyond our powers of endurance, we would get up, push up the chunks, make a good fire, light our pipes, smoke, crack jokes and cuss our luck. The exception to the rule was to see a soldier who did not smoke. The fact is, as a rule we were all pipe-makers, for we would get the root of ivy, saw it into blocks, and each fellow would have something to whittle on as the long days rolled by; and we have seen pipes thus made, with a pocket-knife only, that would lay over any of the briar-roots we have seen in stores for beauty of design and excellence of finish. And when you meet a rebel soldier to-day that don't smoke and don't like a social glass, you can as a rule put it down that he was not in many hard and "sole" trying campaigns. But enough of this, as we must keep moving if we keep sight of the stirring events of those days.

Early on the morning of November 23, 1864, Hood's army was on the move in the direction of Nashville, Tennessee. The heavens above were dark and gloomy. The roads were in fair condition, and the boys were all as gay as larks. All seemed to be rejoiced at the idea that a decisive blow was going to be struck. Pretty soon a blinding snow storm set in, but on we went as cheerful and light-hearted to all appearances as school boys, Forrest's cavalry being in front, and cleaning up the Yankees as fast as he caught up with them. We infantry fellows had nothing to do until we struck the enemy at Columbia, Tennessee, about 16,000 strong, under command of General Schofield. Gen. S. D. Lee strung out his corps as if he was going to sail into them, while Hood with the other two corps of infantry undertook to play Sherman on them by a flank movement. The boys were perfectly delighted with this move. We moved around to the right of the city, crossed the river on pontoons, and lit out for Schofield's rear; and in marching through the cedar brakes and the old red clay fields, it was not long before a fair per cent of our command were as barefooted as they came into the world. The writer marched one whole day with his feet as bare as is the hand penning these lines. But the idea of our flanking the Yankees was such a good joke that we kept going. We remember passing during the day a magnificent old farm house. The good lady and her pretty daughters came out near where our line was passing, and opened up a regular old-fashioned Methodist camp-meeting. They shook hands with the boys as they passed until their arms were as limp as a dish-rag. The old lady finally gave out, and from the greatness of her good rebel heart she said she wished she had a hand "big enough to shake hands with all the Army of Tennessee at one time."

On we went, through farms and by-ways, over hills, through valleys and wading creeks as we came to them, and about two hours by sun we came in sight of the Nashville and Columbia pike at Spring Hill, nine miles in Schofield's rear. All day we could hear Lee's guns pressing Schofield, yet in Columbia, and we just knew that we had him. Just south of Spring Hill was a farm extending up to the pike and the town as well, and our line, Cleburne's Division, was formed at once and moved forward through the field, under a pretty heavy artillery fire from a battery up near the city. But on we went, and when we got in sight of the pike it was lined as far as we could see both ways with a Yankee train of wagons, and it was moving in a hurry, and best of all, there was only a line of Federal skirmishers between us and it. The hearts of the boys beat high with joy at the prospect of getting to "prowl" all these wagons. We were not more than three hundred yards from the train when all at once we were commanded to halt. Our line dressed to the right, and at the command, "Right face, double-quick, march!" we moved off to the right in a run. We had to pass within about four hundred yards of the battery already referred to, and you can bet your high ocean wave that it poured the shot and shell into us "from who laid the chunk." We moved about half a mile to the right, halted, dressed to the left, and at the command, "Left face, forward, double-quick, march!" we went back over the ground we had just come over to a point immediately in front of the battery. By this time it was dark. We were all astonished at our line not being thrown across the pike, capturing this whole train and completely cutting off Schofield's retreat.

Some of the boys said at the time that we were waiting for Bate's Division, which had stopped to bridge the creek we had waded just a little way back.

About an hour after dark, Granbury's brigade was moved forward to the farm fence. We were halted and ordered to lay down. Pretty soon we heard troops moving just over beyond the fence. Some one said: "That is Bates' Division 'tieing' on to our left." Others insisted that they were Yankees. Dick English of General Granbury's staff, said: "I'll be d—d if I don't intend to find out." The boys let down the fence for him, and he went in on his mule. This was the last we saw of Capt. Dick English. He was captured by Henry and Jess Owens, two Federals we met over in Wise County since the war. At this time we were in sixty yards of the pike. We remained here until about ten o'clock, were then moved back about 100 yards, built fires, ate our supper, of parched corn and "biled" pork, laid down and went to sleep; and while we slept and slumbered Schofield's army passed by on its way to Franklin. We were actually so close to the pike, and had such poor guard arrangements that many Federal soldiers came out to our fires as they passed by to light their pipes, and were captured.

Generals Hood, Cheatham, Bate and others, in high places, have said a good deal since the war in trying to fix the blame for this disgraceful failure; but the easiest and most charitable way to dispose of the whole matter is to say that the gods of battle were against us and injected confusion into the heads and tongues of our leaders.

When the morning of the 29th came, cold, bright and frosty, there was nobody there but us. Not a Federal to be seen except a few dead ones. The writer found a Federal staff officer (at least he looked like one from the way he was dressed); he had on a No. 5 pair of Wellington boots, and as his soul had quit this mortal coil and gone up from the field of so-called glorious war, we remarked to ourself: "Well, as we are barefooted, and he don't need those boots any more nohow, I reckon we will take them;" and whether it was for the sin of robbing a dead man, or the sin of putting a No. 8 foot into a No. 5 boot, we paid dearly for those boots, as the sequel will show. We warmed a piece of our cold "biled" pork by the fire, greased our heel and instep, and worked into them. The boys all said we looked nice, and indeed more like a French dancing master than a Confederate soldier.

Pretty soon everything was on the move towards Franklin. The pike was lined with broken-down wagons and bursted-up caissons, everything showing that the Yankees were intensely in earnest in their efforts to get away from us. We hadn't gone a mile until those boots were biting our feet. At the end of the next mile they were eating on them like a litter of hound pups would a chunk of liver. At the end of the third mile we were slashing along with our feet in the upper end of the boot legs. At the end of the fourth mile we walked out of them and on to the pike with bare feet, and O, how the sharp flint rocks on that Tennessee pike did scarify our soles. But then "there is no remission of sin without the shedding of blood."

About three o'clock in the afternoon we climbed the high hills about one mile south of Franklin, and had a fine view of the pretty little city, as it nestled down in the valley, on the banks of the clear, laughing, limpid waters of Harper's Creek.

On the right of the pike was an open valley farm, on the left a magnificent open woodland.

Away to the right, above the city, and across the creek, is a frowning fort. All in our front, extending from the creek above to the creek below the city, is the Federal line of breastworks, and behind the works are heavy lines of Federal infantry, and about 40 yards in front of their main line is a skillfully arranged abattis. This was made from a grove of young trees of white locust that grew hard by. They had cut those trees and laid them in a line with the tops toward us, with each limb trimmed to a sharp point.

Cleburne's Division of Mississippi, Arkansas and Texas troops were to the right of the pike, the left of Granbury's brigade resting at the pike. Gen. Hood and his staff are setting their horses on a little knoll over to the right, and just in rear of Govan's brigade. We see Cleburne, Cheatham, Bate and other generals. Riding up to where they are, we see Hood, and his tried marshals in council. We see them ride away slowly, each to his command, and the word soon comes down the line: "Men, Gen. Hood says we must take those works." The deep, solemn silence that prevails about the hills and down in the beautiful valley is disturbed now and then by a boom from a long range gun, that sends an occasional shell quite to our line. Officers of the line acquaint the men with the direful undertaking before them. They tighten their belts, draw their hats and caps well down over their heads, and at the command "Forward, march!" the long line of Confederate infantry move down the hill and on through the open valley, with banners flying and bands playing our national airs — "Dixie" and the "Bonnie Blue Flag." Gen. Cleburne, on his fine bay mare, leads his division, the lion-hearted Granbury leads his brigade of Texans. When within about 400 yards of the enemy's works the command rang down the line, "Forward, double quick, march!" Gen. Cleburne, with his cap in his right hand, and pointing toward the enemy, put his mare into a run. He was shot dead within about 100 yards of the works. Gen. Granbury was killed about the same time. This advance and charge came nearer measuring up to the pictures of battle we see in the books than anything we saw during the war.

Our men went through the abattis and right on over the enemy's main works, but our line was so weak it could not hold the position, and those that were not captured fell back just outside of the enemy's works, and with our men on the outside and the Federals on the inside, the battle was kept up until about 1 o'clock in the morning.

About this time the enemy retreated towards Nashville, about twenty miles away. Our loss in officers and men was terrible. Our brigade went in with 1,100 bayonets, and only 460 men answered to roll-call the next morning. The writer walked on the battle-field, and having already described in these chapters as best we could the field of Chickamauga, we will abridge this by saying we saw where blood had flowed along the sewer by the pike like water. We saw Confederates near the works who had been struck by hundreds of balls after they were dead.

About 10 o'clock we moved on toward Nashville, but the heart of the grand army of Tennessee was broken. Why Hood made this fight, when he could have flanked the enemy out of their position in three hours, is a mystery that will be satisfactorily explained when we all shall have crossed to the other side. Gen. Hood was doubtless a brave, good man, but he lacked a great deal of being a military genius.

## CHAPTER XXIX.

TRYING DAYS AROUND NASHVILLE — THE GREAT BATTLE DECEMBER 14TH AND 15TH — DISASTROUS RESULTS — THE RETREAT — OUR MULE, "KICKING JIM."

After a day of weary marching we arrived in the neighborhood of Nashville late in the evening of December 1. The country around the city, especially on the south, is a semi-valley, hilly country, yet a very large per cent of it was in farms, orchard, gardens, vineyards, etc. The line on which our brigade was placed was a high, open field. From it we could see the spires, domes, parapets and minarets of the capital city of Tennessee, with all its indications of wealth, ease and comfort. Around about the high points of the city on the south were many forts and "oodles" of big, black-mouthed cannon pointing our way. The weather was bitterly cold. First came a snow-storm, and then a "misting" rain, freezing as it fell. Here the mechanical genius of the boys was called into use in providing winter quarters. Some constructed very clever places to sleep in out of corn stalks. Others built houses in the shape of an old-fashioned chicken-coop, out of rails, and covered them with dirt, and when the boys would bounce out early in the morning to answer to roll-call, their dens would be steaming like a bed where an old sow and a litter of pigs had roosted over night. The writer knows whereof he speaks, he having been promoted to the honorable position of adjutant of a regiment, and it was his duty to take in the morning report of those present and absent. Our feet were in such a condition that we could not wear shoes, and we had them tied up in pieces of blanket. Our regimental headquarters were down in a ravine in rear of the line, and Maj. Tom Broughton's, the new commander of the brigade, was just over the way in a cluster of great oaks. The question of fuel was a serious one. The farm fences were of cedar rails, and when we would build a fire of them it would blaze up, snap and pop and jump away like fleas, and there would be nothing remaining but a black spot on the ground. Our rations consisted of unbolted flour, pork and beef.

About the 12th the writer and Capt. James Selkirk, acting Lieutenant-Colonel, made application for a two days' leave of absence and as it had to go to corps headquarters only, it was approved and returned on the 13th. He had a mule and the writer an old, long, lean sorrel horse. We lit out for the hilly country in our rear at once. The ground was covered with snow. The first night we stopped with a very clever, generous old farmer. He gave us good coffee, fresh butter and ham and eggs for supper, and a big, fat feather bed to sleep on; the same for breakfast, supplemented with fried chicken, and a Jeff Davis bumper of Robinson County whisky as a prelude.

We put in the whole of the 14th in foraging around promiscuously over the country, gathering up "sox," shoes, boots, clothing, tobacco, in the hand or in the plug, to carry back to the boys.

That night we stopped with a man named Culberson, and he treated us as though we were lords in the land. Seeing that we were clothed and yet had no shoes on our feet, he took his boots from his own feet and presented them to the writer. His intentions, of course, were good, but those boots came very near costing us our life, as will appear later on.

At two o'clock on the 15th our leave of absence expired by the law of limitation, and we must be at our command by that time or be subject to suspension as officers absent without leave. At twelve o'clock we were at the burying ground of the Patterson family. It was some eight or ten miles south from Nashville, and from the names of the Pattersons on the tombstones, they must have been burying them there for the last two hundred years. From here we lit out for our command. When we arrived the battle was raging with terrific fury, and had been for two days. We soon found the boys. Maj. Tom Broughton had fallen by the way, and Capt. James Selkirk, commanding our regiment, was put in command of the brigade, he being the ranking officer, and as the writer was his adjutant, he went up with him and was in the position of acting assistant adjutant-general, a powerful big jaw-breaking title for a fellow to put on all at once, and doubtless but for the circumstances surrounding we would have swelled like the toad in Æsop's fable. The snow had melted and the earth in the old fields was as soft as mush. In less than two hours we were ordered to charge the enemy. We drove them back. Our line was just to the right of the Nashville and Franklin pike, and Bate's division of Tennesseans to the left. About three o'clock we were moved onto the pike and marched off in the direction of Franklin. All this time Bate's Tennesseans were having a battle royal with the Yankees. The roar of musketry seemed to be greater than any we had heard during the war. All at once a big, mounted negro fellow came dashing down the mountain from the direction where the battle was raging. The writer caught the bridle of his horse and made him give up quite a lot of Ned Buntline's works. We were marching along at the head of the brigade, beside Commander Selkirk, examining our capture, and inwardly enjoying the prospect of having lots of good reading when the battle should end. While at this, Capt. Selkirk nudged us in the side and said, "Look, Wilkie" (for that was the nick-name he called us by), "we are whipped." We cast our "eagle eye" over to the right and up on the mountain field, and sure enough the Confederates were running like wild cattle, throwing everything away that would in the least impede their flight. About this time the enemy run a battery upon the pike and sent a shell about every two seconds down just to the left of our line, screaming like the damned in purgatory, plowing up the earth and spattering us with mud. This put our boys on the run for the first time during the war.

About this time a long, slim Tennessee mule came running diagonally towards the pike. He had been slightly wounded and was running for dear life. As he passed us we made a leap for him and caught in the piece of rope around his neck. He ran with us some 200 yards, down through a field, our feet touching the ground now and then. When he reached a plank fence that ran off at right angles to the pike, he reared up on it with his fore feet, and while in this position we climbed on to him. We gathered up the slack rope, got our heels well fixed in his flanks, and then made a motion at the side of his head opposite to the pike with our hand, and he "lit" down on a run for the pike, working his ears like a Texas jack rabbit getting out of the way of the hounds. The broad pike was full of wagons of every description, and the team drivers were whipping and slashing in every manner imaginable to get away. Our mule would sail through between the lead and wheel horses, back and forth, yet we " sot " as close and tight as if we had been a part of him. On either side of the pike were the foot people. Our mule would " swipe " them down platoons at a time, and time and again we heard them say: "Shoot that blasted feller on the mule." This did not alarm us in the least, for we much preferred being shot by our own men to going to a northern prison — we had " been there, Eli." About dark we struck Brentwood, a little station in the mountain where the railroad passed through, and as we passed a telegraph pole we slid down off our mule and wrapped the end of the rope around it. The stop was so sudden that he changed ends so abruptly his tail popped like a whip. He looked at us with his big brown eyes, with his ears pointed forward, in great astonishment. We told him that on closer acquaintance we would like each other better.

Here we found Gens. Hood, Forrest, Ross, Chalmers and all other Generals who had not been captured making a desperate effort to rally the "people," but they would walk around

"SHOOT THAT BLASTED FELLER ON THE MULE."

Hood and all the other big officers just as if they had been common mortals. A great big fine-looking young fellow on Forrest's staff charged up horseback, with a bright, shining ivory-handled pistol in hand, to where the writer and his mule were, and demanded in tones of authority, "What in mischief are you doing here?" We caught his eye, and pointing to the men throwing away their guns and running for dear life, says we, "Do you see those people?" He looked and said, "Yes." "Well, me and this mule are just like them — whipped and tempestuously demoralized, and are trying to get away." We saw a big smile spread over his face, and with a twinkle in his big blue eye he said, "Hold on to your mule." We assured him that nothing short of death in the pot could separate us. Now, this may be regarded by some as rather a compromising position or condition for an Acting Assistant Adjutant-General in the Rebel army to be found in, but as we started out in these reminiscences to keep in the neighborhood of the truth, we let it come cold and pure when we do say anything. However, the reader must bear in mind that we are not telling all we know.

Pretty soon the remnant of Granbury's brigade came up. By this time the idea of making a stand at Brentwood had been abandoned, and the boys were walking like they had a thirty days' furlough in their pockets and were bound for home. The fact is, Hood's army, except Ector's Texas brigade and the cavalry, was merely an armed mob; and the reason of the morale of Ector's men being worth anything was because it had been guard for the pontoon train, and missed the great battles of Franklin and Nashville. Every fellow seemed to think he was his own commander now, and marched to suit his own notion — one, two, three and a dozen, in a bunch. We kept no company that night except that of our mule. On we went, but could find no good place to stop. After a while we came to Franklin. We crossed the creek, passed on through the city, by the battle ground, and away out south of the city found a battery camped. We slid down off our mule, tied him, spread our blankets, crawled under a caisson and fell asleep. When we awoke the next morning we found it to be Douglas's Texas battery. The boys were not long in rustling up a pair of bits and cotton rope enough to make us a bridle. Hard by was a farm-house, but the people were off somewhere South for their health, or up North inspecting prisons and rations. Anyway there was no one at home, and we borrowed a saddle we found sitting on the porch. We now had a bridle, saddle, blanket and mule, and about 100 miles of good running ground between us and the Tennessee river, with about 150,000 wild and wooly Yankees trying their dead level best to catch us, and Gen. Grant never threw his leg across the back of Egypt, or Gen. Lee his across that of Traveler, when either felt prouder than the writer did when he got on to the hurricane deck of that mule, with his business end towards the Yankees and head pointing down the big road towards the lower lands of Dixie. Here is another point where we paused long enough to jaculate. "You can bet yer high ocean wave!" we felt primin' good. We rode leisurely along, waiting for our foot "people," having no other thought than that they were many miles in our rear, when it is a gospel truth that they had walked four miles further than we had ridden the night before. When "Kicking Jim" and "me" got to where the boys were they gave us a grand reception.

By this time a cold, damp-sort of rain had set in from the east, and it poured down just like it knows how to pour over there in Tennessee, and three great armies, with all their transportation, having marched over the pike inside of a month, is a sufficient guarantee of its being in a wretched condition; and oh, how horse flesh, mule flesh and human flesh did suffer! Our teams were very poor and our men were poorly clad. We saw men marching in that slush and ice with their feet as bare as the the naked truth, and men wounded and on crutches trying to make their way south; and the Yankees seemed to think that the safety of the government at Washington, and that the liberty of speech and freedom of the press might remain upon earth, depended on their keeping us on the run night and day. On the high hills south of a creek, about four miles north of Columbia, we made a stand. By this time we had somewhat recovered, and we gave them a fight that convinced them there was a good deal more to be done beside catching us. But there were so many of them they soon flanked our position and sent a galling fire right down our line. This was more than human nature could endure, especially when our feelings were all broken up and we were on a dead run for a safe place. Our line began to break, when that brave officer, Capt. Ben Tyus, of Corsicana, said: "Lieutenant, rally the men." We moved around and said all we could under the circumstances, for to tell the whole truth, we were glad to see the men leaving, for in a half an hour longer we would have been billed for a northern prison. In our slashing around trying to rally the men we found Curg Smith, now of Denton, standing at the bottom of a sink-hole at least twenty feet below the surface of the surrounding grounds. We commanded him to come out and get in line. He looked up, and his eyes looked more like two recently washed big turnips on a black stump than anything we could then or can now compare them to. Pretty soon we were all on the move, and besides being very anxious about our safety, we were marching through a cold rain, the drops of which emphasized their striking us as if they had been so many drops of burning grease. About dark we arrived at the pontoons across the river, near Columbia. It was here Gens. Cheatham and Forrest passed some hot, unladylike words about whose corps should cross first. Our recollection is that Cheatham gave way. We crossed over and camped in the beautiful city of Columba, using yard-fences, shade-trees, or anything else we could lay our hands on to build fires to keep us from freezing.

## CHAPTER XXX.

THE RETREAT ATTENDED WITH MANY HARDSHIPS — WAYNE COUNTY, TENNESSEE — GEN. CHEATHAM HAS FISTICUFFS WITH A PRIVATE SOLDIER — CROSSED THE TENNESSEE RIVER — A FEW DAYS AT CORINTH, MISSISSIPPI — AT TUPELO, MISSISSIPPI — ORDERED TO NORTH CAROLINA — THE BOYS DO UP MONTGOMERY, ALABAMA, ON THE WAY.

The morning of the 17th opened up freezing, cold and clear. The next stand we made was at Pulaski, Tennessee, the home of that great general, polished gentleman, and successful railroad man, John C. Brown. We remained here a part of one evening, one night, and until about 10 o'clock the next day. We were now approaching that part of Tennessee — "Wayne" and some other counties — where bushwhackers did much abound, and hatred for the Southern Confederacy did much more abound; therefore we did not forage around loose over the country much, but kept pretty well together, and in the middle of the road. The earth was frozen as hard as a buck's horn, which made traveling a little better. However, our poor teams were continually stalling in that mountain country. We remember on one occasion when a commissary wagon was stuck tight and fast, Gen. Cheatham came riding along and took in the situation, and as he lit from his horse he said, "Here, boys, let's roll her out; our grub is in this wagon," and suiting his action to the word he put his shoulder to a wheel and lifted until his face was as red as the flannel lining of his gray overcoat. About this time a long, hungry-looking, sad-eyed Confederate, like the high priest, "passed by on the other side," as good as to say, "If you want that wagon out get it out the best way you can. I am too busy now pulling my own freight to the other side of the turbulent waters of the big Tennessee, to spare the time to monkey with a wagon stuck in the mud." This was too much for impetuous Cheatham. He grabbed a camp kettle from the feed box and struck the fellow flat between the shoulders with it. The lick could have been heard half a mile. The fellow took it good-naturedly. We enjoyed the show as " Kicking Jim and me " viewed it from a safe distance on the hill-side.

On the 24th we arrived in the neighborhood of a small burg on the Tennessee river called Bainbridge. Here we formed a line to fight the Yankees at least hard enough to keep them back until the pontoons could be laid across the river, and the securely laying of those pontoons across that great river, right on the Mussel Shoals, where the waters were rushing and bounding, causing each bridge to buck and hump itself like a Texas mustang, was a feat in civil engineering or bridge building that the school-boys will read about many years after the Confederates are all gone and say, " Well, this knocks the socks from Cæsar's bridge across the Rhine."

On Christmas morning while it was yet dark we crossed over, and when we struck the high hills on the south side we looked across at the hills beyond and said to ourselves, "Tennessee, good-bye, we like ye, because it was in your borders our sweet blue eyes first saw light, and feasted upon the magnificent beauties of the far away Blue Ridge; and besides all this, thou art the

Volunteer State, the abiding place of Robertson County whisky, and the home of Andy Johnson and Bill Brownlow." While we were in the midst of these pious, soothing sort of private, home-made reflections, boom, boom, goes the big guns on an ugly Yankee gunboat down at the foot of the shoals, as good as to say, "If I could only climb these shoals."

Right here we pause, fill our powhattan with Duke's mixture, touch a match thereto, and lean back in our easy chair, and remark in as near our own language as we know how, "You can bet your other high ocean wave" that we felt a good deal better.

That day we arrived at the city with the big spring, Tuscumbia, Ala., the home of the father of our first Brigadier-General, Deshler. Our brigade was detailed to do provost-guard duty for the city, and not many hours had passed before the boys had a bountiful supply of pork on hand. We were too old a soldier to make any inquiry as to where they got it. This was the first of this kind of duty we had ever struck, and though the city was a mere mock of its former beauty and greatness, and the country around as lean as a summer coon, so far as being good foraging grounds was concerned, yet we enjoyed this service.

About the 5th of January, 1865, we were moved down to Corinth, Mississippi. The country from Tuscumbia to Corinth had been the raiding grounds for both armies from the early days of the war, and it was the most dreary, barren, wasted, God-forsaken looking country we have ever seen. The few people remaining in it seemed as a rule to hate a Confederate soldier about as bad as they did a Federal. The country could not have looked in much worse plight had it been subjected to so many raids by wild Comanche Indians, and when we arrived at the city of Corinth there was nothing to be seen there that was encouraging. Even the women had so far fell from their patriotism of the earlier days of the war that they "let up" on shaking white handkerchiefs at us, as much as to say "We wish you Godspeed." The armies of Sidney Johnston, Grant, Beauregard, Buel, Price, Grierson, Forrest, Van Dorn, and last of all, Hood's broken army, were there, and the people had seen to their fill the empty foolishness of the so-called "pomp and circumstance of glorious war."

We are now within four months of the last days of the Confederacy, and as we approach these sacred precincts we remove the shoes from our feet and with uncovered head walk the corridors of the charnel house of the buried hopes of four million people, whose deeds of heroism and matchless powers of endurance will live in history, poetry and song when the wings of time shall have grown weary from the flight of centuries. But in giving a history of the reckless deeds of those of our army whose hopes had been changed by the fortunes of war to desperation, we shall continue to walk in the middle of the road, and give as true a statement as possible of the incidents as printed on the pages of memory quite thirty years ago.

One cold morning about the 20th of January our army was out on the move for Tupelo, Miss., the infantry marching on the railroad, and those on horse or mule back traveling the dirt road. Kicking Jim came in good play now because the boots that Mr. Culberson gave us away back yonder at Nashville had quite ruined one of our feet. They were about three sizes too large, made of half tanned leather, and as impervious to water and grease as a cow's horn. A wrinkle in them had eaten a hole on top of our right foot. It poisoned and inflamed a place about the size of a silver dollar, with a dark gristle place in the center. We cut a round hole in the boot to fit it, and when we mounted our mule the boys wrapped our foot and leg up as best they could with pieces of blanket. Capt. Tom Kemp, of the 7th Texas, and the writer were traveling together. About two o'clock in the afternoon we stopped at an old-fashioned double log house with a hall between, to warm. While here the writer had a chill and high fever, all from the pain in our foot. The big, fat, blue-eyed, motherly lady of the house insisted that she untie our bandages and do something for it. We were very positive in our objections to her meddling with it, because of being ashamed for her to see our dirty foot and the remnant of a pair of socks we had on. Her good husband came in pretty soon and they prevailed, and when they unwound the rags down to our boot they found that it had swollen until the affected part protruded at least half an inch through the hole already referred to. The good farmer with his knife cut the boot off, and in less time than we have been writing the last ten lines, our foot and ankle had swollen to frightful proportions, was in a high state of inflammation, and the outlook was indeed flattering for us to lose a leg, if not our life. The good woman laid a big pillow on a chair and our foot on it, and after a free application of warm water and soap with her own hands, she made the biggest slippery elm poultice we ever saw and wrapped the foot and leg in it, and then stowed us away in a good bed and tucked the cover about us as only a woman can; and notwithstanding the condition of our foot, we felt like we didn't want to be disturbed for the next 300 years.

About nine in the morning she awoke us, and upon removing the poultice we found the inflammation all gone, and our foot and ankle "swunk up," until they had the appearance of having at least two yards more skin than was necessary. We have been thus particular in describing this incident in order that boys and young men may read it and to some degree appreciate the fact that God has scattered mothers, fathers and sisters all over the world. We have found them everywhere. We were able to resume our journey that evening, and reached our command the next day, camped about a mile west of Tupelo. While here the writer made his maiden effort as an Adjutant-General on the report of the doings of Granbury's brigade in the Tennessee campaign. We wrote it on yellow paper with a poor pen and very lean ink. It may be on file with other Confederate documents at Washington, who knows?

It was here the boys went en masse to Gen. Dick Taylor's headquarters and demanded that a reasonable number of men whose homes were west of the Mississippi be permitted to go home on short furloughs. The request was granted. They drew lots and every fifth man went home.

Tupelo and the country around it, like Corinth, bore the marks of fire and sword. Great farms had gone to ruin, and fine mansions where youth, beauty and wit used to meet and "Chase the glowing hours with flying feet," were now the abode of owls, bats and hobgoblins.

But we must move on. January 26th the remnant of the once proud and great army of Tennessee were put on box cars and flat cars and started for North Carolina. The roads were in bad shape, and it was some time in the night of the 28th when we reached Mobile, Alabama.

Reverses in recent battles, hardships and exposure, together with the hopelessness of our cause, rendered a majority of our soldiers a dangerous outfit, and subject to be led on into reckless excesses when led by shrewd, designing men. Mobile escaped being systematically prowled because of our arrival there in the night time, and put on board a vessel early the next morning. The sail up the Tensas river was nice indeed. The banks on either side were as verdant as in spring time. We quit the boat at Tensas landing, and were shipped from there to Montgomery, Ala., on the cars.

We arrived in this fine old city just before sunset, and were marched through it to the neighborhood of the Atlanta and West Point Railway depot. A strong guard was at once thrown around our camp, with orders to allow no one to go over into the city. This of course was the correct thing, but it proved an utter failure in results, for as soon as the boys got through supper they took their guns and pulled out to the city in squads of three, five, and by dozens. They "had it in," first for the provost guard, hospitals rats and fancy post officers, and the city police, and to say the boys took charge of the city and run it for their own account that night would be putting it as we saw it. Everybody was indoors that night in Montgomery except those mad Confederates, and they were making things hum on the outside. The center of attraction was a kind of free-for-all, route step, go easy, beer-jerking place called the "Light House," located a little way down the river. The Arkansas and Texas boys took charge of this outfit, music, dance hall and all, and run it for all there was in sight. Everything ran very smooth and nice until about 10 o'clock, when bad Georgia pine-top whisky got into it. Just across the street, on the bank of the river, a Dutchman had a little grocery store. Some of the boys went in to buy his wares, and he made the mistake of giving them a dram. They soon commenced clerking for him. After a while they told him they could run the business without him staying up and losing sleep. In fact, they told him he would be much safer at home with Catherine and the children. The Dutchman did not stand upon the order of his going, but went at once. The boys then rolled out a barrel of his whisky into a gulch that ran off towards the river, set it up on end and knocked the head out. The first intimation the writer had of what was going on, Lee Kinman, from Denton County, came into the dance hall and blew his breath in our face. We asked him where he got "it?" He said: "Don't ask any fool questions but follow thou me." We followed, and when we got there the boys were drinking out of the barrel like horses or thirsty chickens around a pan of water on a hot summer day. We don't know that, all things told, a soldier is any more liable to get drunk than anybody else, but we do know that if a man undertakes to drink whisky out of a barrel like a horse does water, he is more liable to become slightly off his bearings than if he drank from a glass or bottle. We account for this strange sort of philosophy on the hypothesis that we gauge our drinks by the size of the vessel we take them out of. The last we saw of the boys and the "female women," they were as drunk as lords. Some made it into camp that night, some came in in time for roll-call after daylight. Some had one eye in a sling and some had two. Some didn't have as many ears nor as much hair as they took to town with them. The floor of that dance-hall was a sight to look at, and the anxiety of Pharaoh to get rid of the children of Israel after the ten plagues, was as tame as a "summer's day dream" compared to the earnestness of the citizens of Montgomery to get rid of us, and well they might have been, because if those demoralized soldiers had met with resistance that night there would have been music in the air.

## CHAPTER XXXI.

FROM MONTGOMERY TO BENTONVILLE, NORTH CAROLINA — ON THE WAY THE BOYS "DO UP" COLUMBUS, GEORGIA, AND ACT "VERY UNLADYLIKE" AT FORT VALLEY — GEN. JOHNSTON AGAIN IN COMMAND OF THE ARMY OF TENNESSEE — THE BOYS CHEER HIM.

Pretty early the next morning we were put on board the cars and started for Columbus, Ga. This is another grand old city, and some of the boys had little accounts to settle with it, they having been there in hospital when the post was commanded by a Col. Leon Von Jenkins. They had found that there were lots of "good picking," as they called it, in this city. The railroad was in a dreadful condition. We have seen the rails and ties go down out of sight into the mud and slush as the train would pass over, therefore it required the whole day to make the run.

We arrived at Columbus about dark, and doubtless the good people having heard of our conduct at Montgomery, conceived the idea that our meanness could be headed off by giving us a grand reception. The city seemed to have turned out for the occasion its beauty, with music and oratory. Transparent flags were displayed bearing such mottoes as "Welcome the Army of Tennessee," "Welcome to the Heroes of Chickamauga," "Welcome to the Brave Defenders of our Homes and Fire-sides." They had long tables strung out in the depot, loaded from end to end with nice things to eat. Men were speaking, women were speaking and in their sky-rocket oratory they compared us dirty rebels to the Roman Legions under J. Cæsar, when they crossed the Equator; the Old Guard, under N. Bonaparte; the squad that cleaned up four million Persians at Marathon; the outfit that went all the way to Egypt with O. Cæsar and fanned out M. Anthony and Cleopatra; to those foolish fellows who didn't know what a good pair of legs were made for at Thermopylæ; to Hector and the Greeks who "fit" with the Trojans ten years around Troy because C. Paris stole Helen, the wife of a petty king by the name of Menelaus, and a good deal more that we can't remember now, but it all fell as harmless and ineffective on the boys' ears as the first half a dozen sermons usually do on a congregation at an old-fashioned camp meeting, for as fast as they would fill up on cold ham, chicken, baked pork, pickles, pies, cake, light bread and hot coffee, they would take their guns, form into companies and pull out for the city. The writer would have doubtless been with them, but just as he cleaned the last chicken bone and tossed it over his left shoulder, he made a break for the car he had been riding in, and got a fall that hurt him so bad and made him so sick that he threw up a pile of free lunch as big as a water bucket. The boys helped us to our car, spread our blanket and put us to bed, so that we know nothing of what was done except as the boys told us on the way next day, and from that we feel safe in saying they did the saloons and gambling houses up in an artistic manner.

At noon the next day we arrived at a very clever little city called Fort Valley, Georgia. The good women of the city had turned out in force with well filled boxes and baskets to feed us. The boys behaved on this occasion very well, as a rule, the exception being that some of them took charge of the baskets and acted rudely.

Macon was the next city on our way, and the boys "had it in" for that in great shape, but our train ran through the city at the rate of at least forty miles an hour. However, several of the boys jumped off as the train was running. We arrived at Millidgeville, the then capital of the Empire State, some time after dark, and were turned loose about a mile from the city in the piney woods. The night was dark, damp and cold, and the country was barren of anything we could turn to account as fuel. The writer struck out down a pine ridge in search of something, anything, out of which to make a fire. After a while we found an old, dark, gloomy church, and hard by a graveyard. We ripped the palings from the graveyard fence until we had a bundle about half the size of a bale of cotton, and with it on our shoulder we started back. From where we were we could see a flickering light away down yonder in the pine thicket. Of course we steered directly for it, and walked off into a red clay gulch and fell about forty feet. The palings rained down on us for half an hour at least. We looked up, saw the stars, knew we were not in purgatory, and that the government still lived at Richmond.

Here we struck the line of Sherman's march to the sea, and the railroads all being destroyed, we had to foot it across the country to a point about a half day's run by rail from Augusta. The march across Sherman's track will never be forgotten by " we uns " that made it. We have ofttimes heard the expression, " as poor as a church mouse," and the scarcity of everything in the way of something to eat for man or beast in that belt measured up to the full meaning of " poor." The country looked as wild and wierd as if the abomination of desolation had waltzed through it with fire in one hand, sword in the other, hell in its heart and lust in its eye. Everything was gone, and the tall brick chimneys stood cold like Druid sentinels marking the spot where the fine old mansions once stood. We had no transportation, and each fellow carried his clothing, bedding, cooking untensils and rations and when it would rain and get our luggage well soaked, it was a pretty good load to carry, and we would sink into the Georgia clay half leg deep; but we were as hard as pine knots, and could stand anything.

About the 20th of February we arrived at Augusta, Ga., late in the evening. It was here the writer paid $75 for a tin cup of sweet milk and a dodger of corn bread. By this time the boys had cooled off, and were well disposed, as a rule. Some of the boys remained in the city overnight and worked it pretty well, while the bulk of our command crossed over the Savannah river on the long bridge, passed through old Hamburg, and camped in the "moaning pines" on the soil of South Carolina. We have now crossed the line of Sherman's march, yet the gloom that had settled on the face of all the people, and the evident early demise of our Confederacy was marked on everything. Even the people of South Carolina let up on giving us encouragement. Once in a great while, on a march through the State, a woman would wave a white handkerchief at us, which used to cause us boys to scream like wild cats and toss our gray caps into the air; but misfortunes, mistakes, bad management and the failure of having carried out our first intentions of whipping ten to one, and keeping up the lick until we had thrashed the United States and the outside world thrown in, had caused the "rebel yell" to die in our throats, and we would not be comforted, because we had sad eyes, weary legs and empty stomachs. Our fare was lean indeed. The day we arrived on the banks of the Tiger river the writer carried Jim Hardin's gun, ammunition and luggage while he would go miles out on either side of the road in quest of something to eat. Late in the evening he came in, not having found a thing. The writer was now commanding Company "B" and had just five men in his company, and we all started out on a foraging excursion, and the only thing we found in all that country was an old sow, solitary and alone. She was a powerful big frame but very poor. We slaughtered her, and after taking her hide off, the middlings were about as thick and tough as your shoe soles, and had about the same amount of grease in them. When we put the meat on to fry we would have to put on the skillet lid to keep it from jumping out. We made supper and breakfast on it, put the remainder in a sack, and the boys took turns in carrying it until we ate it up. When a fellow would get tired you would hear him say, "Here Jim, I am tired; it is your time to carry Grandmother awhile," and so on.

We were now kind of hanging on Sherman's flank, but at a safe distance, for there were so few of us that we could not have lasted until we were all gone had we got in his way. We stopped some days near Newberry. While here Newt Millhollon and the writer put in one rainy day foraging. Early in the morning we crossed quite a little river, and on we went from house to house. Quite all the white people had quit the country, leaving the negroes in possession. In some instances the negroes had moved out the fine furniture of their masters into their own houses. We saw a fifteen hundred dollar piano sitting in an 8x10 negro kitchen, and the little darkies playing around and on it like monkeys. During the day we gathered some half a dozen canteens each, of molasses, several bushels of yam potatoes, a couple of hams and other truck. We were loaded down to the guards, but we could "tote" as much as a mule and travel as far with it in a day. Night caught us out. It had been raining hard all day. It was dark, and we were pulling for camps guided by the reflection from our camp fires. The river already referred to was up booming. We had forgotten all about crossing it, and when we came to it we thought it was a big sheet of water in the road, like those we had waded. Millhollon walked right into it with a bushel of potatoes, six canteens of molasses, a ham of meat and other truck swinging around his neck, and but for sticking his fingers in the stiff red clay banks and pulling he would have gone down to the bottom like a chunk of lead. He pulled himself out and remarked: " Why, that is the blasted river we crossed this morning." He was thoroughly scared; we could hear the beating of his great, good and honest heart as we helped him out. We found a bridge and crossed over safely, and when we reached camp the boys put in a good portion of the remainder of the night cooking and eating.

The next day we were moved out, and rounded up next at a pretty little city called Chester, S. C., and recollections of this place are not as sweet as honey. It was here the writer made application at a big fine mansion hard by where we were camped, for a dry place to sleep his company of five men, and had to put ourselves by force into a negro kitchen. The cold February rain was falling in torrents, and oh, how cold it was!

On the morning of March 2nd we were put on board the cars and landed at Greensboro, N. C., about 2 o'clock on the morning of the 3d. The clouds had all gone by, and it was cold and crisp now. On the 4th we were shipped down through the beautiful city of Raleigh to Smithfield, in the turpentine region of the State. As soon as the train stopped we could hear the boom! boom! of cannon away off to the right down in the swampy, turpentine lagoon country about old Bentonville. We knew that Johnston and Sherman were at it again. The sound was familiar. We arrived on the battlefield about 10, a. m., on the 5th of March, and as we marched to our place in the line of battle we passed near where Gen. Johnston was standing, and the boys cheered him lustily — the first thing of the kind we had witnessed since the beginning of the campaign in Tennessee under Gen. Hood.

The main battle of Bentonville had been fought the day before our arrival and Johnston had set Sherman back on his haunches, and he resorted to his old tactics — flanking.

We walked over the battle field on the 5th, and found dead Federals whose knap sacks were filled with that of which they had plundered the citizens on their march through the country. We remember examining one who had his filled with silk dresses, silk stockings, and other articles of ladies' apparel.

Mr. M. Collins!

Your description of the last Confederate days about Bentonville, Raleigh and Goldsboro are delightful to read. I'm glad you've given your experience to the public. Those were stirring times, and I knew your descriptions are true to life — and full of the quiet humor of truth.

Yours truly,
Melville D. Landon
Eli Perkins.
208 West End Avenue New York

## CHAPTER XXXII.

STIRRING DAYS ABOUT BENTONVILLE AND SMITHFIELD, NORTH CAROLINA — REORGANIZATION OF THE GRANBURY'S BRIGADE — THE ARMY MOVES WESTWARDS — GRANBURY'S BRIGADE FINDS A BARREL OF APPLE BRANDY — ALL HANDS AND THE COOK GET ON "A HIGH LOANSOM."

Under almost any other commander but Gen. Joseph E. Johnston, the Confederates at Bentonville, N. C., would have become demoralized at once; but the rare exception to the rule was to find a man that did not have implicit confidence in Johnston's ability. His lines here were in the shape of a horse shoe, with two ugly, muddy, deep creeks in his rear. These were spanned by two frail bridges. Sherman kept pressing our line all round on the outside. About noon on the 6th it began to rain. About three o'clock in the afternoon, Gen. Schofield's corps of infantry made a desperate effort to capture the frail bridge, and thus cut off our only line of retreat towards Smithland and Halifax Court House, and would doubtless have succeeded but for the gallant conduct of Gen. Tom Harrison's brigade of Texas and Arkansas cavalry. Here was an instance of cavalry charging and driving heavy lines of infantry. Granbury's brigade relieved the cavalry. W. J. Lacey, of Denton, was in this charge and had his horse killed. Gen. Hardee's son, who had joined the 11th Texas cavalry, was killed here. Later on in the evening our brigade was marched across the first bridge and on across the second. There were only about 160 of us, but each man was a whole column by himself. We were strung out about forty feet apart, and went to fortifying the deep, coarse sand. We were not long in getting pretty good holes in the ground. Our line was at right angles to the creek, extending from it across the big road, over a sandy ridge, to a deep swamp on our left.

The clouds rolled by, the big moon came out, and the drops of rain yet on the deep foliage around looked like millions of diamonds. We slept quite snug that night.

The morning of the 7th opened as nice and

bright as it possibly could in that God-forsaken country. Not a gun to be heard. Everything in that deep, wild wood was as quiet as a May morning. The boys had hung out their wet blankets to dry. The writer walked some yards up near the bridge to deposit some luggage in an ambulance. All at once a heavy fire of small arms broke loose over across the creek. We thought it was only the boys discharging their wet guns, and we felt fretted at their wasting so much good ammunition. All at once here comes a company of Confederate cavalry dashing over the bridge, and on they go on a dead run up the big road towards Smithland. The road forked right at the bridge, the one turning immediately down the creek and the other running off towards the east or Virginia. We knew at once that those fellows had found something over there, and were not riding for their health. Our educated military eye discovered at once that the bridge had been covered about two feet deep with pine tops and sand, and that lots of people and things had crossed it the night before, and sure enough the whole of Johnston's army had crossed it that night, passing within 200 yards of us, and we knew nothing about it. The Federal infantry came over at once and cut our little brigade off, running us into the big swamp already named. We all got out and struck the big road in squads away on towards Smithfield, but we were a sight to behold — all covered with that black, murky mud. But we were as cheerful as larks, "Johnson was in command." We set fire to a lot of those resin-bearing pine trees, and were soon warm and dry. We all nearly wore ourselves out chewing "rosum." It was the first time we had ever found it in bewildering profusion, and we just chewed like sheep. While in this section our gambling went on night and day. Fires made of those big, fat pine-knots gave lots of good light, and we would sit around on the ground in squads of two and four, and stack up our Confederate money at poker like lords. Money was plentiful, but there was nothing we could buy with it. Our rations consisted of bean crackers, some bacon, some beef and some cornbread, and not having any soap, and sitting around those pine-knot fires, we certainly did resemble a lot of Creek Indians going on the war-path more than the flower of the southern army.

Gen. Sherman seemed to be content to rest a few days on his victories, and slid off down towards Goldsboro, while we went into camp and reorganized. The 15th Texas Regiment was made into two companies. Lieut. J. L. McCracken, late of Fort Worth, and the writer were tendered Captain's commissions.

The writer declined because he had it in his head that he had earned a Colonel's commission. The line of promotion having been closed against him by reason of his Captain being on post duty at Tyler, Texas, and having commanded a company a good share of the time for three years, he felt that nothing short of three stars on his collar would do. So we made application to the Secretary of War at Richmond for a Colonel's commission for ourself, a Lieutenant-Colonel's commission for Cage Harris, and a Major's commission for Gus Schneider, of San Antonio, with authority to raise a regiment of North Carolina Confederate buck negroes. This may seem pretty desperate, but we were in desperate circumstances, and were in for any port in a storm.

We would have succeeded in getting the commission and in raising the regiment but Sherman spat on his hands and commenced pressing us. Lee abandoned Richmond and the Confederate government was put on wheels and headed towards the setting sun, while Gen. Stoneman had crossed the Blue Ridge from Greeneville, Tennessee, and was heading us off, while Sherman poked it to us in the rear and flanks.

Gen. Johnston moved his army leisurely on towards the west, up through Raleigh, and towards Greensboro. The infantry could have marched fifty or sixty miles each day, but the bad roads and the poor condition of our teams made the getting along with our artillery and other trains a very difficult matter.

On the morning of April 15th we camped on a nice piece of woodland somewhere between Raleigh and Greensboro, cleared off the grounds nicely, stretched our dog tents as if we were going to rest quite a while. The writer was standing at the head of the street we had made by our tents on either side, when he noticed a big, handsome, blossom-eyed fellow by the name of Maxwell, coming out of the pine thicket, carrying a camp kettle. He beckoned to us to come. Says he, "Smell in the kettle." We smelled. It was about half full of apple brandy. We turned it up, drank as long as we could hold our breath, caught

"CAUGHT IT AND DRANK AGAIN."

it and then drank again. The third breath was expended in the question, "Where did you find it?" He pointed over towards the pine thicket. By this time the boys were going that way in crowds. We followed on, of course. When we got there the boys had raised the forty-gallon barrel of apple brandy from the hole in the ground caused by the wind having blown a great oak tree up by the roots, and some old North Carolina fellow had used it as a grave for his pet barrel of brandy, which he was saving for his own use when the cruel war should end, to be used when the day of rejoicing should come when the Southern Confederacy had been acknowledged by all the nations of the earth as a power that had won its independence by the patriotism of its people and the prowess of its soldiery in battle, and had demonstrated the fact that they were capable of self-government. But be all this as it may, we can say with confidence that few barrels of brandy have ever made a more jolly crowd than ours was on that occasion. In a very short time the bulk of our brigade was "over there" around that barrel. By general consent the writer was appointed to issue it out. A faucet was soon made from a boot-leg, cut to fit and twisted into the bung-hole. Then commenced the drawing of it off in canteens and camp kettles, and each canteen must need run too full, and rather than pour it out so the stopper would go in we would drink it. The truck was so exillerating and self-esteem elevating, that it was not long until we concluded the service was menial. We resigned the position and lit out for the camps. All hands got drunk. Even our chaplain, the Rev. Hayes, a very excellent man, got as drunk as an "English lord." The effect of the fluid extract of apples on the mental and physical outfit of the writer was such that he cannot keep in the middle of the road in an effort at describing what the boys said and done during the remainder of that day and night. Our own experience is all we can give.

Along in the afternoon there came a big rain. When the big drops commenced striking us we looked for our dog tent. Looking with both eyes there seemed to be two of them, shut one eye, and there would be one tent. With one shut, and taking aim with the other, we made a dive and went through to our waist at the other end. We were too weak in the privilege to get out or back and, therefore, just lay there, and the hard cold rain pelted us good while we sucked the water from our little blonde mustache and cooled the fire the apple jack had already set up within.

The next morning we were a hard looking set, and for the boys we plead as an excuse for this spree the peculiar surroundings. We were just at the threshold of the dying days of the Confederacy, and we had received that morning the news of the assination of President Lincoln in Washington by J. Wilks Booth. Referring to the last named incident it was very natural for a large majority of the boys to rejoice at the news, while a few wagged their heads and said they feared it portended bad luck and hard times for the South, and history has demonstrated that they were right, for Lincoln was doubtless an honest conservative man, and was a greater man than the Republican party, and had he lived, the reconstruction of the Southern States would have been effected without the people of the South having to pass through so many years of missrule and down right robbery. But enough of this; we must keep our line of unwritten history.

While here our very dear friend, our mule, "Kicking Jim," put in his appearance, having been marched across the country from Tupalo, Miss. Jim looked a good deal worse from wear, but was glad to see us. We sold him for $275, in new issue Confederate, and then gave the $275 for a No. 12 pair of English jack shoes. These shoes like our boots already referred to, were history makers and will figure in these chapters later on with a pair of home-made woolen socks that a Quaker woman gave us.

Our army seemed to be moving leisurely along. We knew nothing of what was going on, the boys all seemed to be content to leave the management of affairs to Gen. Johnston, but a deep feeling seemed to prevail that the days were big with events, but we put in all our time when not on the march, or out foraging in betting at poker, seven-up and chuck-a-luck.

We had oodles of money, but there was nothing in the country it would buy. The only thing we found in North Carolina in superabundance that could be had without money or price was good " chewing rosum."

## CHAPTER XXXIII.

THE LAST CONFEDERATE DAYS — SURRENDER AT GREENSBORO, NORTH CAROLINA — WE GET OUR PAROLE AND ONE SILVER DOLLAR — MARCH ACROSS THE BLUE RIDGE AND AT GREENVILLE, TENENSSEE, THROUGH THE CAMP OF 15,000 ENRAGED NEGROES — A DREADFUL WRECK ON THE E. T. & V. RY., — NARROW ESCAPE.

About the 25th of April we went into camps near Greensboro. By this time the report of Lee's army having surrendered to Grant had become a settled fact in the minds of all. However, the boys were yet content to leave all the matter as to what should be done to Gen. Johnston. We were ready, to a man, to start with him in the desperate undertaking to fight our way to the Trans-Mississippi Department, but Gen. Johnston was brave enough and good enough to do the right thing, and surrender to Gen. Sherman on very fair terms. We boys all walked up to the place designated, signed some sort of a document, got our parole, and one dollar apiece in silver. We were not required to stack arms nor to ground our arms in the presence of the enemy. The fact is, we did not see a Federal soldier during the whole proceedings. Many of the boys left their guns in the woods where we were camped. The writer drove his little Confederate sword out of sight into the earth, and it is there yet if some North Carolina farmer has not plowed it up.

The struggle was now over, and we felt relieved after so many years, months and days of waiting and watching suspense, and early on the morning of the 3d of May, we started for our homes in the West, a cheerful, light-hearted set of soldiers enjoying the consciousness of having done our whole duty.

At Saulsbury we were allowed to elect which route we would go home by, the southern route, via Atlanta and Vicksburg, or across the Blue Ridge to Greenville, Tenn., thence by rail to Nashville and by boats to New Orleans. A large majority of the Texas and Arkansas troops elected the northern route. The writer and his company of five were with them. We were permitted to march at will, but it was understood that we keep pretty well together, in order that we might draw rations. Greenville, Tenn., we knew, was due west from Saulsbury, and at about 300 miles distance.

Our road ran up the Cataba river, and through a fine country that had not been eaten out by soldiers. We traveled in squads of twos, threes, fives and dozens, either in the main road, or off on either side of it.

The writer on this three hundred mile walk paired with Newt Millhollon. Some days we would quit the big road and travel settlement roads all day, always keeping our faces towards the west. Sometimes we would round up with the command at night, and sometimes we laid out. We fell on this plan to get plenty of grub and other things we had been short on for lo these many days; and it worked to a queen's taste. We would eat from three to eight meals a day at the tables of these good North Carolina people, and it got to be no surprise to us to run onto a bountiful supply of moonshine whisky.

On we go, up, up, and up to the top of the Blue Ridge, and camp one night in Swananoa

Gap, right at the headquarters of the classic, rushing, bounding, seething, foaming, mountain-bound and rock-ballasted French Broad river. The reader may think we are extravagant in using so many double-geared, high-pressure adjectives in our reference to this river. You would change your mind, however, and say, go on in the use of them to the end of this chapter, if you could only see that wild, woolly, weird country, with mountains piled up so high that it requires two men to see to the top of them; the French Broad dashing between for forty miles, down grade, against, over and around rocks as big as the Capitol building at Austin. Away up near the head of this river we found the beautiful, clean, well-watered city of Asheville, and it was here that the writer swallowed the first bitter pill of all the doses we had to take in being "reconstructed."

The city was under martial law, and a regiment of Federal negroes were on provost duty. We soon noticed that the citizens were sly and exceedingly cautious in favorably recognizing us as we passed along. Out in the western part of the city we noticed two elegantly dressed ladies standing on the front porch of a nice dwelling some forty yards back from the street. They started down the walk so as to be at the gate as we passed. We raised our cap as one of them presented us a bouquet of flowers as large as a dinner bucket, but just as we were putting our ex-Confederate hands on it, and our heart was nearly jumping out at our mouth, a big, burly buck negro stuck his bayonet to our bread basket and remarked like one with authority, "I guess I'll take dat," and he took it. This brought to our eyes the first tears we shed over the grave of our buried Confederacy. We soon dismissed the matter from our mind, when the thought occurred to us, "Guess this is as good as you deserve, after three years of making trouble 'with the best Government the world ever saw.'"

On we go down the road, overhanging mountains to our right and the river to our left, now and then striking a valley of one, two, three or five acres, and apple trees old enough and large enough to fill up the whole valley. At last we came to Paint Rock. This is a perpendicular ledge of limestone, so high that we had to scream at the top of our voice to read "Take Humbolt's Buchu," painted in letters near the top.

Here we quit the river and strung out over the hills towards Greeneville, some ten miles or more away. We camped early in the afternoon some three miles out from the city; a brass band of some thirty pieces commenced playing, and people for miles around on those East Tennessee knobs came rolling in, men, women and children. Some would draw near, while others, fearing some of those big horns might burst, remained at a safe distance.

About 8 o'clock a young, bright Federal lieutenant came out on horseback to pilot us into the city. He marched us through the camps of about 15,000 armed negro soldiers. Their new uniforms, mounted with all the burnished brass they could stick on to them, looked exceedingly black, tall and war-like. Their guns, with bright, shining bayonets, were stacked on each side of the road. They gathered in lines just back of the guns, and they were mad all over through and through, because they believed that our little squad of Confederates were individually and collectively responsible for the death of their temporal savior, Abraham Lincoln. For a mile or more we walked the gauntlet under every abuse that horde of infuriated armed negroes could turn their tongues to and heap upon us. Our boys were smart — they kept their heads up, eyes to the front, did not return a word, and walked in the middle of the road. The writer walked near the Federal lieutenant who had come out to meet and escort us in. He rode with his pistol in hand and didn't say a word, and his face was as pale as the paper we are writing this on. He evidently appreciated the perilous situation we were in. On we go, down through the city, right by Andy Johnson's old tailor shop, and into camp on the woodland hills beyond. This was the second dose of reconstruction pills. We believed then that the plan had been laid to have these infuriated negroes murder us all, and twenty-seven years has not changed our opinion. It could have been done and in the then condition of mind of the people of the North, they would have approved it, as a meet and proper offering to the offended gods for the taking off of President Lincoln, a thing with which we had no more to do than the man in the moon. We give it just as it occurred; be your own judge.

We remained here two days, but steered clear of the city. However, the writer and his side partner went to see the home of Andy Johnson, and the house where John Morgan was betrayed, captured and murdered. We here saw the first negro school taught by a woman who was at least white on the outside. This we note as reconstruction pill No. 3, and the boys began to get pretty hot under the collar, and were not very choice in the language they used in expressing their opinions of the way the Yankees were doing things, and as spies and short-hand reporters were with us all the time, noting everything we said, it began to look like our chances for going to a northern prison were very promising. We were joined here by quite a number of western men from Lee's army, and by the time we were ready to start there were two train loads. While at the depot some of the boys went down to the engine to take a look at the engineer. When they came back their report was: "We are going to have it to-day, boys." "Why?" asked some one. "Well, Jackie is as drunk as a biled owl." We were put in box-cars, improvised seats by a plank on blocks down the center, on which we sat like chickens on a bean-pole.

At the signal to start Jackie pulled his steam

manipulator out to his full capacity, and our train went forward with a bound, while we all piled up in the rear end of the car. Pretty soon our train, in the lead, was dashing through farms, woodlands, deep cuts, over high grades and short curves, bouncing on the rough track like a bucking mustang pony, and raising clouds of dust, and from the hilarity of the boys they all seemed to say, " let her go, Gallager." There were about as many riding on top as inside the cars. The writer was sitting between two Federal soldiers, trying to read a new Louisville Journal, but the attempt was as much a failure as if it had been printed in Egyptian hieroglyphics. All at once we felt an extra shaking quiver of the car. We looked out at the side door and saw the engine and tender yet on the track and going down the road, while the half dozen cars ahead of ours were going end over end down an embankment. Just at this instant our car stopped still. From where we were it looked to be a high grade, but as a matter of fact, it was the tops of tall trees we were looking at instead of the green earth, our car having come to a standstill on a bridge which was at least seventy-five feet above the bottom of the creek. We made a leap for life forward and lit on the bridge, where it rested on the stone pier, a Confederate at the same time jumped from the top of the car just ahead of ours, and struck the writer just as we were gathering for the second leap, and knocked us back. This steadied us. He missed the bridge and went over. We stepped forward and saw him as he went down. He lit astride of a syacmore sappling that had grown so close to the pier that it leaned outward, and it let him to the ground unhurt. The wreck was a fearful sight. After gathering up the wounded and dead we found thirteen who had gone through the war, and who a little while ago were full of hope and joy at the prospects of once again crossing their own threshold, and pressing to their hearts the loved ones they had left at home. But their great good and brave hearts were still in death. With the wonderful facilities at the command of the Government for handling wrecks, it was not over two hours in setting everything to rights and on we went.

About twelve o'clock the next day we ran up to a small station called Mouse Creek. Our train was yet in front. While the crew were at dinner we filled our canteens with water and about fifty of us got on top of the car so as to get a good view of the country that evening as we ran through low East Tennessee. The writer was especially anxious for a look at the country, as it was on Mouse Creek he was born and lived until about a yard and a half high, and we should like to have stopped there and travel a few days over the hills and through the valleys where we spent our early boyhood, wearing a long tow shirt, and learning war by fighting yellow jackets and seed ticks; but as Union bushwhackers were giving afternoon matinee, for the benefit of such friends as wanted to start new graveyards, and as ex-Confederates were in pressing demand as subjects, we thought that our chances would be better with the Comanche Indians as neighbors on the frontier of Texas, than near the home of our childhood.

## CHAPTER XXXIV.

ANOTHER WRECK AT MOUSE CREEK, TENNESSEE — A SMASHUP ON THE RAILROAD NEAR TULAHOMA — AT NASHVILLE THE AUTHORITIES THREATEN US WITH THE PENITENTIARY — ON BOARD A BOAT — WE ARRIVE IN NEW ORLEANS AND HAVE A ROYAL TIME GENERALLY.

Standing on that car indulging our well trained imagination in these pleasing reflections, the whistle of the train in our rear commenced to blow, and it kept on blowing. We all knew it was running away with the engineer, and it was coming down those three miles of down grade with a vengeance. Here it came like a living monster, wild with rage, and plunged into the rear of our train, knocking things into "smithereens." No one was killed, but several Confederate limbs were broken.

They were not long in getting things in shape again, and on we go, down through Calhoun, Charleston, Cleveland, and as we pass through Tunnel Hill the shades of night were spreading over the valley of Chattanooga, while the summits of Lookout Mountain and Waldron's Ridge were tipped with golden sunlight. Our run from here to Nashville was made without anything occurring that was exciting, except when our whole train quit the track in a deep cut somewhere between Tulahoma and Wartrace. This happened in the night-time. Our recollection is no one was hurt. The boys by this time were getting pretty badly out of humor, and were not very choice in the language they used in expressing the opinion that the United States were trying to kill and cripple by railroad accidents those of us who had not fallen in battle; and indeed it did look kind of suspicious.

While in this sort of humor the boys were very extravagant in their description to the Federals of what we were going to do for them when we got home to Texas and joined Kirby Smith.

The authorities kept shorthand reporters with us all the time, noting all these threats. We arrived at Nashville about 1 o'clock in the afternoon. Here the writer inquired of an old negro woman as to what she had in her basket, by calling her "Aunty." We thought for a time a big buck negro would crawl our hump in spite of us, before we could apologize for not calling her a "colored lady." This we note as pill No. 4 in our reconstruction medicine.

After a little while we were formed in line and marched off in an entirely different direction to the one in which we expected to go. This created some uneasiness in our minds, and when the head of our column bluffed up right at the door of the penitentiary, our worst fears were confirmed. The boys looked at the great iron gate, the high gray walls, and the sentinels walking their posts, but no man said a word. We all looked wild and felt weak.

The silence was broken by Jim Hardin, of Wise County, when he blurted out the inquiry, "Boys, what in thunder do you reckon all this means." At this we commenced gathering in squads and talking low, and when a fellow would turn and look at those high rock walls the white in his eyes seemed to increase in amount and the color of blood would leave his face. But no man could be found who could or would tell us what we were there for; all we could do was to judge by appearances, and they held out nothing on which we could hang a hope. Every now and then some fellow who had been extra loud in his threats as to what he intended to do when once in Texas, would say, "Let them bring their durned oaths. I'll take all they have got of them." To put it short they kept us there about two hours in this terrible suspense, but it cured the boys of talking too much and loud with their mouths, and served to take more of the salt, pepper and vinegar out of us than almost anything we had struck.

We were then marched up through the city down to the river and on board a steamboat. We were as jolly as larks, and happy as big sunflowers, not only because we were alive, but also at missing such a good opportunity of being put in the Tennessee penitentiary. Pretty soon our boat pulled out down the beautiful Cumberland; this style of traveling was the richest thing we had struck. Plenty of good rations, good place to sleep, and a fine healthy opportunity to play cards, and lay plans for the future for no one knows how blank one feels, but a soldier who has had his wants provided for for years by the strong arm of government, and all at once thrown onto his own resources.

The trip down the Cumberland, the Ohio and

on the heaving, swelling, palpitating, muddy bosom of the Father of Waters was without incident or accident, save a little scrap the writer had with a freckled-faced, hamelegged, Federal soldier. He was one of the mean kind who was fully possessed of the idea that Jeff Davis and all our Southern leaders should be hung as high as that fellow who was after Mordecai's scalp and "failed to cut her," and the common rebel soldier should be disfranchised, and his knife and tobacco taken away from him. Several of us Confederates were lying around on the hurricane deck, "sunning," when we foolishly allowed ourselves to be led into an argument with him, and, as might have been expected, the argument waxed not only warm, but got hot, hotter, hottest. He made some extravagant assertion. We disputed its correctness. He came back at us with the lie. We sailed at him with our fist, and he at us with a "Charge bayonets," and we were glad when the boys interfered and prevented him from gigging us up and tossing us overboard, which we believe was in the heart of the scoundrel to do. We were young then, and knew but little of the philosophy of controlling our temper. We were wild with rage, and as blind as a rattlesnake in August. We went into the cabin, then down on deck, and as we stepped over a camp kettle the boys had scaffolded upon something in which they were boiling beans, we tilted it over, filling all the extra space in one of our English Jack shoes with thick, boiling soup. Our first impulse was to jump overboard into the water. The danger of being sucked in under the side-wheel of the great steamer took that idea out of our head. We sat down, untied our shoe, and when we removed our thick sock the skin from the "bosom" of our right hind leg came with it, even down to the thick skin of our heel, and while we were hopping around all over the deck, suffering with pain, the engineer stepped up and insisted that we put a coat of oil and white lead on it, from a bucket hard by. We sailed at him for a fight, thinking from the blue clothes he had on that he was another mean Yankee, and only wished to get us poisoned, but we have since learned he was right in the remedy suggested. We will offer him an apology when we meet on the camping grounds beyond. But for that red-headed soldier who got us into all this trouble we have no very hard feelings. A quarter of a century has cooled us off, and besides, he doubtless belonged to the home guard or militia, and thought it smart to insult a prisoner.

At a fort below Memphis our big boat landed for coal. While here the negro soldiers came down by thousands. We remained on the boat, but the negroes seemed very much out of humor, and said a great many hard things to us. We felt pretty safe, and held our own with them pretty well.

While at Memphis all the Arkansas troops got off. The parting was pretty trying. We had been together in the same division, "fought in the same field; slept in the same tents," in all the campaigns of the Army of Tennessee.

The next landing was at the mouth of Red River. Here all the East Texas boys changed boats for Shreveport and Jefferson.

Our next landing was at New Orleans. We were marched out into the city and halted on Canal street, near the Clay monument. In this grand old city we struck in rich profusion everything that enters into the list of a soldiers' living, that makes him happy and at peace with all the world.

By this time our numbers were reduced to about one hundred and fifty. While we were awaiting orders, a smart, slick Scotchman by the name of Jim Walker, who belonged to our outfit, made some sort of a dicker with a big Scotch restaurant keeper hard by to feed us. The eatables and drinkables were simply royal in quality and quantity. Later in the evening we were put on the march down toward the French quarter of the city. The writer, because of his lame foot, fell behind. A Frenchman by the name of Vinette stepped up and said, "Hello, my good fellow, you seem to be having a rough time of it. Put your arm around my neck, and I will be your 'crutch' until you get to your quarters." And by the time we got there the Frenchman and the writer were staunch friends. There seemed to be a natural affinity between us, and before bidding us good evening he invited us to come up to his house, which was only about four blocks away, and take coffee with him the next morning. We were quartered in the second story of a large brick, a very nice place. We had not been there an hour until the women, God bless them! commenced coming in with baskets filled with clothing and good things to eat, and by noon the next day you would have had to draw a fine bead on your own messmate to determine who he was. The boys were all dressed up, shaved, had their hair cut, and were shampooed until they did not look like the same fellows.

We kept our promise, and went to see our Frenchman; and when we entered his door the big, broad sheen of sunlight on the face of his fat blue-eyed jolly American wife made us feel at once that we were at home, and had found another one of the mothers God has located in so many places on this beautiful earth. In her sweet presence we felt at perfect ease.

A Frenchman's coffee means something good for breakfast, and for their nice attentions we have been wearing Vinette and his "gude" wife in our heart of hearts as jewels all these long years. Should these lines fall under their eyes, we tender them our heartfelt thanks, and should they not, we will make it all right "when life's fitful fever's over," and we meet in the "City beyond."

On our way back we passed a big grocery concern. The proprietor insisted that we come in, remarking that he "had something inside." He piled quite a lot of hams, canned goods, sugar, coffee, etc., on the counter. We thought he knew that we were there a paroled prisoner, out of money, and not able to buy a breakfast, and that he was poking fun at us. We were not long in telling him that nothing but our lame leg kept us from giving him a genteel thrashing for thus insulting us. We felt ashamed when the good man told us that he intended to give it all to us, not as a matter of charity, but he felt that he was due us every kind treatment at his command, because we had "borne the heat and burden of the day," while he remained at home and made money. We were good friends from that time on. Come to find out, the people of New Orleans had opened their doors to us, and we were their royal guests. Barber shops, street cars and everything else was ours to use at will and pleasure.

About 2 o'clock in the afternoon finely-dressed ladies commenced coming into our quarters. About every fourth Confederate could play some on the violin. We soon had all the instruments needed and then commenced the dancing, old-fashioned, new-fashioned and fancy. The boys of the 6th Texas were from Matagorda. They, with a few San Antonio fellows of the 15th, could do all the round dancing, while we grass-fed North Texas fellows were knocking the living daylights out of an old Virginia reel. The weather was warm, and the way the boys did drink ice lemonade, dance, sweat and smell sweet, was making up for lost time. This was part of the programme each day from 2 till 9, p. m., when the negro guard would "pipe" lights out and "us in."

## CHAPTER XXXV.

INTRODUCED INTO THE FAMILY OF DR. HAMILTON — FIND OUR OLD FRIEND DAN M'GARY — EAT A FINE DINNER UNDER VERY EMBARRASSING CIRCUMSTANCES — THE TRIP OVER TO GALVESTON AND HOUSTON — AT HOME AGAIN.

Through our friend Vinette a party of us, consisting of Col. W. A. Ryan of Austin, Maj. J. A. Farmwalt of Granbury, Lieuts. Mark Kelton of Galveston, Chase of Georgetown, and the writer, were introduced into the family of Dr. Hamilton, a very wealthy man. The family consisted of the doctor, his wife, and two charming daughters, Miss Sallie and Miss Mary, living in a fine old mansion, furnished in royal English style. Of course we went. We were ushered into the doctor's private parlor, or more properly speaking, his private sideboard or saloon, for it came as near being a completely furnished, elegantly fitted up little saloon as anything else, for in the way of good things to drink and smoke it was a dandy.

The first thing the Doctor did was to "set 'em up," and when we threw our head back and opened our shoulders to let the oily old whisky run down, with our eyes "pointed" skywards, what do you think we saw? Why it was nothing more nor less than a great big, silk, sure enough silk, Confederate flag, tacked overhead to the ceiling. Just at this time in came his good wife and two pretty daughters. We were introduced and the show went on.

The Doctor, of course, was master of ceremonies and would suggest a toast before each drink, naming the speaker. Drinks were in order at the conclusion of each game of euchre. The writer did not feel at perfect ease. Being quite a young man, and having been raised on the frontier of Texas, it was the first thing of the kind he had struck, and therefore he kept himself in the background as much as possible. After about the fourth round at the sideboard we were sitting on a big lounge, when Miss Sallie slung herself down by our side, almost covering us up with her breezy dress, furbelows and flounces, causing our heart to bounce up into our neck, almost choking us. We swallowed it back and replied to the shower of questions she rained at us the best we could. We were very uneasy for a while for fear some of the things we felt crawling under our shirt would get on her, but after one more toast we felt like the negro did when the white man asked him to take a drink with him, "If you can stand it I can," so we sailed in and told her " of moving accidents by flood and field, of hair-breadth 'scapes in the imminent deadly breach, of being taken by the insolent foe and put in prison, of my redemption thence, and with it all my travel's history. These things to hear did Miss Sallie seriously incline, and bade me if I had a friend that loved her I should but teach him how to tell my story, and that alone would woo her."

By this time we were full of joy, but the hour was late and we must needs go. When we returned to our quarters who and what do you think we found? A dispatch announcing the fact England had acknowledged the independence of the Southern Confederacy? No. That Lee had whipped them again in Virginia? No. That the Yankees were not going to send any scallawags and carpet-baggers down South to eat up the substance of our people? No, not that by a brutal Democratic majority. But it was our old friend in the early days of the war, Dan McGary, now of the Houston Evening Age, the only Simon-pure Democratic paper in the world. He had laid a door shutter on two barrels, spread his blanket thereon, and was lying sound asleep, with his Dan Webster face being kissed all over by the soft silver rays of a Southern moon. We awakened him and asked him what he was doing there? He said that the war in the Trans-Mississippi Department was too tame for his blood, and that in an effort to get east of the great river where he could share and share alike with the boys in the "pomp and circumstance of glorious war," the Yankees had picked him up, and what there was left of him was there.

Dan was not a graceful figure in the whirl and bewildering mazes of our afternoon dances, but when it came to swinging those pretty, dreamy Creole girls, he was a column of his own height, and a whole brigade from "who laid the chunks?"

Our days in New Orleans were full of pleasure. Our circle of acquaintances widened every day. Business in the great city was booming, and all the boys were tendered positions in dry goods, grocery, commission or banking houses. We were exceedingly popular with all classes, and all the boys had sweethearts.

Dr. Hamilton had made the writer a present of a nice hat, coat, pants, boiled shirt, clean socks and some pocket change. One day Prof. Chase, the leader of our band, and the writer were invited to dinner, at the Doctor's. We went down quite early after breakfast. On our way there lived a rebel barber who insisted every time we passed his place that we drop in and let him fix us up. On this occasion we were quite anxious that he make all the improvement in our appearance possible, as we were going to spend the day with our best girl, Miss Sallie. He made our hair as stiff as a board and as black as a crow with some sort of cosmetic, while our little blonde mustache was twisted into horns as sharp if not as stiff as a rat-tail file. When we arrived at the Doctor's Miss Sallie answered the bell and went with us into the parlor. Chase went to the big, fine piano, while Miss Sallie and "us" stowed ourselves away in a big bay window. She laid a pillow on a chair and our burnt foot on it;

and while Chase played she fanned our foot, and the courting went on. Pretty soon Chase took French leave and left Miss Sallie and the writer alone together, and how we did court, and chat of the nice time we would have in the sweet bye-and-bye.

Away along in the evening, nearly the time when we had been used to having supper, dinner, was announced. We felt a little nervous when we entered the fine dining room, and our military eye flashed on the fine table furniture. Having been raised on the frontier of Texas, it was but natural for us to feel "out of whack" in the presence of so much finery and so many things to eat. Miss Sallie occupied a seat to our right, the Doctor at the head of the table, his wife at the foot, and Miss Mary just across the table from us. We were helped first to soup and fish. This we cleaned up as quick as a litter of hound pups could have done it. The doctor next loaded our plate with fish, flesh and fowl. This disappeared as mysteriously as the other. He loaded it the second time, and it went the way of all the earth. By this time we were right on the frontier of the province of pastry. We sailed into it with "letters of marque and reprisal" and hauled into port all that was put in our reach. All at once our stomach, which we thought was like a sink-hole, and could not be filled, sounded the alarm, and said it could not and would not hold any more and there was no use sending any more down. We felt full. The big veins in our neck swelled up, and great drops of sweat trickled down our back. The Doctor now inquired as to our favorite wine, and we didn't know the name of a single brand. He noticed our confusion, and suggested his choice. This of course we dropped on as ours. He emptied about half a bottle into a big goblet that was about half full of chipped ice and passed it over to us, and we gulped it down, wine, ice and all. This put us to sweating in good shape. We could feel the sweat running in great drops down our back and down the sides of our face, and as we knew the French cosmetic was making black streaks, we perspired the more. What to do was the question of great pith and moment. We had no handkerchief, and it was the first time we had ever struck a napkin, especially with a silver ring around its waist. There it lay. We looked at it and then at Miss Sallie. Finally we made a dive for it, skinned the ring off and gave our

"WE GULPED IT DOWN, WINE, ICE AND ALL."

face and neck a thorough rubbing, and then slyly laid it down on our lap. It was as black as our new cloth pants. We owned up that we had all the dinner we wanted, that a June day in New Orleans was too hot for us to eat much, anyhow, and if the Doctor would excuse us we would get out where the fresh air could strike us. Miss Sallie went with us to the parlor. We told her we had not been used to all that sort of fine fixings; that out in Texas we did not sit and eat for two hours, nor did we starve ourselves until six o'clock in the evening and call the meal dinner, but that we twisted our wheat dough around a stick, held it over the fire, with our beef on another stick, and then ate as we ran.

Miss Sallie and the other members of the family seemed to like us more because of our honest simplicity than anything else; anyway these wild breaks did not "break any squares" between Miss Sallie and us, and we were a regular visitor at her house twice every day from that time until word was received that Gen. E. Kirby Smith and the other boys had quit making trouble with the "best government the world ever saw." But they never succeeded in roping us into another state dinner.

When we left there about the 10th of June, a good many of the boys' sweethearts went with them down to the steamer on which we were shipped to Galveston. On the way around on the Gulf we struck quite a storm, at least it seemed so to us land-lubbers. Dan McGary and the writer had a berth on the hurricane deck, between Texas and the wheel house, and as the great steamer would rock from side to side we would slide from Texas down to the wheel house and from the wheel house back to Texas. As we would make these gyrations we would hold to Dan's big ears. He had a pair as large as W. G. Brownlow, of Tennessee, used to support.

We landed in Galveston about the 12th, and were shipped by rail to Houston the same day. At Houston the ladies gave us a fine supper. The Grand Lodge of Masons was in session, and all the boys who were Masons were invited to seats in the Grand Lodge. Here we met several old friends, among them W. G. Veal of Fort Worth, and W. O. O. Stanfield, of Wise County. The latter furnished us a seat in his buggy, and we traveled with him from Miliken, then the terminus of the H. and T. C. Railway, to Decatur, where we arrived on the 25th day of June, 1865, having served in the

Rebel army three years, three months and twenty-five days.

It is all over now, and the scenes of those stirring days have gone glimmering like the "tale of an hour," a "story that is told," or a school-boy's dream. And while many good men lost their lives, logic is with us when we say a great sin had been committed, and "without the shedding of blood there is no remission of sin." And when a few more fleeting years have swept by, all the actors in this great drama will have joined the silent majority. And when the thunder tones of the last trump shall shake the hills, rock-ribbed and ancient, the blue and the gray will wake up from the fields of Manassas and Murfreesborough, Chickamauga and Gettysburg, Shiloh and Petersburg, Nashville and Sharpsburg, Atlanta and Seven Pines, Jonesboro and Arkansaw Post, Oak Hill and Franklin, Pea Ridge and Fort Donaldson, Belmont and Fishing Creek, New Hope Church and Chattanooga, Mansfield and Bentonville, and with Generals Lee and Grant, Sheridan and Stuart, Hancock and Hood, Johnston and Sherman, Kirby Smith and Banks, Thomas and Taylor, Bragg and Rosecrans, Brown and

Hooker, Burnsides and Bate, Ross and Rosseau, Longstreet and Franklin, Hill and Howard, Hardee and McPherson, Cheatham and Curtis, Pemberton and Porter, Custer and Fitzhugh Lee, Semmes and Farragut, Maury and Wainwright, all, all in bright uniforms, will strike hands in friendship on the beautiful shores of the "land o' the leal," where fellowship will be complete, and love and allegiance by all to one great head is based in the universal fatherhood of God and the brotherhood of man, and we will learn war no more forever.

And the heroic verse of the sainted Father Ryan, priest and poet, will be set to the music of the spheres:

> Furl that banner, for 'tis weary,
> Round its staff 'tis drooping dreary;
>    Furl it, fold it, it is best:
> For there's not a man to wave it,
> And there's not a sword to save it,
> And there's not one left to lave it
> In the blood which heroes gave it,
> And its foes now scorn and brave it —
>    Furl it, hide it, let it rest.
>
> Take the banner down — 'tis tattered,
> Broken is its staff and shattered,

And the valiant hosts are scattered
    Over whom it floated high.
Oh! 'tis hard for us to fold it,
Hard to think there's none to hold it,
Hard that those who once unrolled it
    Now must furl it with a sigh.

Furl that banner, furl it sadly —
Once ten thousand hailed it gladly,
And ten thousand wildly, madly,
    Swore it should forever wave.
Swore that foeman's sword could never
Hearts like theirs entwined dissever,
Till that flag would float forever
    O'er their freedom or their grave.

Furl it, for the hands that grasped it,
And the hearts that fondly clasped it,
    Cold and dead are lying low,
And the banner it is trailing,
While around it sounds the wailing
    Of its people in their woe.

For, though conquered, they adore it.
Love the cold, dead hands that bore it.
Weep for those who fell before it,
Pardon those who trailed and tore it,
And oh! wildly they deplore it,
    Now to furl and fold it so.

Furl that banner! true 'tis gory,
Yet 'tis wreathed around with glory,

And 'twill live in song and story,
    Though its folds are in the dust,
For its fame on brightest pages,
Penned by poets and by sages,
Shall go sounding down the ages,
    Furl its folds though now we must.

Furl that banner, softly, slowly,
Treat it gently — it is holy —
    For it droops above the dead:
Touch it not, unfold it never,
Let it droop there, furled forever,
    For its people's hopes are dead.

www.ingramcontent.com/pod-product-compliance
Lightning Source LLC
Chambersburg PA
CBHW031858220426
43663CB00006B/670